Hundred Thousand Rays of the Sun

Hundred Thousand Rays of the Sun

The Sublime Life and Teachings

of a Chöd Master

H.E. Lama Tsering Wangdu

Translated and Edited by

Joshua Waldman & Lama Jinpa

Published by Lulu.com, 2008 first edition.

www.lamawangdu.org

Cover Design by Lama Jinpa; Photo insert p. xvi through p. xx, Michael Smith; All other photos credits unknown.

Library of Congress Catalog-in-Publication Data

Hundred Thousand Rays of the Sun / Lama Tsering Wangdu; Translated and Edited by Joshua Waldman and Lama Jinpa.

ISBN 978-0-557-00409-6

1. Buddhism, Tibetan 2. Biography

Dedicated to the long and vibrant life,
Of the maroon robed crazy-wisdom Conqueror,
Chodpa Tsering Wangdu Rinpoche.

Single mindedly benefiting the sick and the dead,
Like a mother who holds no sectarian view,
He looks after all people's happiness and cures their pain.

With a hundred thousand rays of the sun,
That dispels the darkness of our egocentrism,
May his altruistic activities spread in ten directions.

Contents

Editor's Preface

I hopped into a Kathmandu taxi in the summer of 1998. It was a typical Kathmandu summer, hot and sticky, and the dust in the air nearly painted out the distant snow mountains in a gray wash. Time was running out for me to find a research subject for the study program that had brought me to Nepal. After several futile attempts to find a subject, I'd heard about the great Chöd master Lama Wangdu who lived on the other side of town. All I said to the cabbie was, "Take me to Wangdu Lama, in Jawelekyel." The taxi driver took me right to the Lama's front door (not an easy task, given the maze-like streets of Kathmandu). But many Nepalis and Tibetans in Kathmandu know of Wangdu Rinpoche, and many of them have visited him. Very few Westerners can say the same.

To this day I can see the look on his face when I asked him about the project. He looked up into the sky, considering my request. Relaxing his gaze and focusing again back on me, he replied, "I'll tell you everything I can remember."

Wangdu first put on robes after receiving Chöd initiation from his root guru, Naptra Rinpoche, when he was just 20 years old. In Tibet, his lama counseled him that there was no need to take the traditional monks' vows, because he was such a strong practitioner. But he was told that it would be suitable for him to wear robes because of his strong role in the community.

"It has been forty years since I've seen my lama," Wangdu told me then. "Since then I have carefully followed his instructions. I am still practicing what my lama taught me forty years ago." He was separated from his guru – and his entire family – when he left his homeland on pilgrimage to Nepal in 1958. After the Chinese invasion of 1959, which sealed the borders, he was unable to return. The lama to this day still wishes to once again re-visit his birthplace.

In traditional Tibetan biography or autobiography, the teachings are embedded in the example of the master. What follows in this book is a traditional autobiography, told in the Lama's own words.

I consider this a rare and precious privilege to share with you. Lama Wangdu has changed my life, and I hope that through this story, he can change yours as well.

—Joshua Waldman, Chapel Hill, North Carolina, 2008

Acknowledgments

If it were not for Pam Gay and the University of Wisconsin-Madison College "Year in Nepal" program, this work would never have been written. I'm grateful for the opportunities afforded me during this fascinating year away from home.

To Tinley Thundrup, Michael Smith and Ngawang Tenpel for their support and encouragement.

Introduction

This book is about a journey through two landscapes. One takes place in a time, culture and lifestyle that are now part of an increasingly distant history. Here, we can follow the adventures— sometimes frightening, sometimes hilarious—of a young Tibetan lama traveling through the fertile valleys and forbidding mountains of the Tibetan hinterland in pre-Chinese Tibet. The other journey is about the clarity and compassion required to bring spiritual training to each sacred moment of our lives. The experiences and lessons of this path are as accessible and relevant today as when Lama Wangdu first strode out into the frosty Tibetan air, some fifty years ago. These two journeys intersect within the context of his spiritual practice called *Severance* or Chöd. This book is also supplemented with clear and direct teachings on this practice.

Chöd is an extensive system of meditation and ritual, using sacred instruments, music and mantras. As a spiritual practice, it is rightly famed for its ability to transform the mind and heart, and awaken individuals to their full enlightened potential. Chöd means "to cut", since both the path and the goal is to cut away the shackles of our fixations, egocentricity and dualistic grasping. Its twin pillars are Skillful Means and Wisdom. The first involves the development of unceasing generosity and compassion. The second is the eventual understanding of the true nature of the selfless, unborn fabric of reality, from which we—and all phenomena— arise. Chöd continues to be a living tradition, with unbroken transmission stretching from ancient times to today's modern masters. Chöd is a well traveled, though steep road to full enlightenment, as well as a powerful vehicle for helping others.

Cultural Setting

Chöd holds an important place in the culture of Tibet and the traditions of Buddhism. It is practiced extensively in monastic communities of various lineages. It was also the mainstay of many wandering ascetics and solitary yogis or Ngakpas, who roamed the mountains and plateaus of the Himalayan kingdoms of Tibet, Nepal and Bhutan. Brought to full fruition by the great female saint, MaChik Labdrön, Chöd has a strong and lasting appeal for women practitioners, who have had a significant impact on its development and preservation. Over the millennia, many traditions and styles developed, especially within the Kagyu and Nyingma sects. Chöpas also play an important role in the community, with rituals for healing, averting misfortune, weather control, pacifying conflicts and guiding the journey through the after-life. Chöd practitioners were known to have wandered the Himalayan landscape, correcting imbalances in the earth and environment, working for both their own realization and the benefit of sentient beings, human and non-human, whose number are as limitless as space.

Chöd in the West

Far from being a cultural curiosity, the central meaning and purpose of Chöd has special relevance for today's world. Many Western students of Buddhism have now been exposed to various lineages of Chöd, and great living masters of these traditions regularly grant the appropriate initiations and transmissions for entry into the practice. Lama Wangdu, however, is unique in being the living holder of the Shijé lineage, brought to Tibet by Padampa Sangye. This great Indian yogi is acknowledged as one of the greatest influences and teachers of MaChik Labdrön, the founder of the system of Chöd. Wangdu Rinpoche keeps these traditions alive and flourishing, both at his monastery in Nepal, and in his frequent visits to the West. When back at his home base in Katmandu, he tirelessly sees dozens of visitors daily, who seek healing from his blend of powerful ritual, spiritual blessings and realized energy.

In the end, Lama Wangdu's pilgrimage is about living life as an impeccable spiritual warrior. Continually bringing a sacred view to his activities in the world, he is the "fool on the hill," whose actions are not driven by personal strategies and the ego's balance sheet of profit and loss. His greatest weapons are an unceasing flow of compassion for all beings, and an unassailable certainty in the true spiritual nature of life and of mind. In these simple, direct stories, we also read about our own life's journey, traversing the wild and sometimes terrifying domains of our material and psychological landscape. How we face these challenges is both a test of our wholeness and an opportunity for further growth and discovery. This biography invites and entices us to live authentically, as life's mysterious adventure unfolds.

—Lama Jinpa, Santa Monica, 2008

List of Key Terms

Brahmin   A high Hindu caste
Butter lamps   A lamp filled with butter or oil, usually placed on the shrine as an offering
Cham   Sacred dance
Chang   Rice beer
Circumambulation   To walk around an object as to show it respect
Damaru   Ritual drum
Dhal   Lentil soup, a staple food in India and Nepal
Dharma   The teachings of Buddha, one of the three jewels
Dzi Stones   A bead stone of mysterious origin; market value for ancient beads can easily reach into thousands of U.S. dollars
Dzogchen   lit. Great perfection, the central teachings in the Nyingma order
Empowerment   An empowerment is a ritual in Tibetan Buddhism that initiates a student into a particular Tantric practice
Gelugpa   One of the four major orders of Tibetan Buddhism
Geshe   An equivalent to a PhD in Buddhist philosophy
Kangling   Human thigh bone trumpet
Kata   A ceremonial scarf
Khampa   One from Kham, an area in Tibet
Long Chen Nying Thig A systematic explanation of Dzogchen within the Nyingma school of Tibetan Buddhism, revealed by the great scholar and adept Jigme Lingpa (1730-1798)
Mahasiddha   Meditation adept who has achieved some level of power through their practice
Mahayana   lit. The great vehicle. Often used in the book to refer to any teachings not of the Tantrayana, or Vajrayana
Mala beads   Prayer beads
Mani Stones   Stone with the mantra "OM MANI PADME HUM" carved on it

Naga	A serpent-like creature
Nyingma	The oldest order in Tibetan Buddhism
Offering Ceremony	See Tsok
Parinirvana	lit. Final enlightenment, the death of the body
Pranjaparamita	lit. The perfection of wisdom. Refers to the core teachings of the Mahayana
Puja	A religious ceremony
Pureland	A type of Buddhist heaven
Rakshi	A hard alcohol usually made from rice or millet
Ransom Torma	An effigy made of roasted barley flour, used to represent the afflicted in order to draw the harmful spirits away from them
Rinpoche	A title of respect for a lama from whom one has received teachings
Shunyata	Meaning "Emptiness" or "Voidness," a characteristic of empirical phenomena arising from the fact (as observed and taught by the Buddha) that the impermanent nature of form means that nothing possesses essential or enduring identity
Stupa	Buddhist monument or reliquary
Tamang	An ethnic group of Nepal
Tantrayana	An extension of the Mahayana philosophy, primarily concerned with meditation techniques
Thanka	A scroll painting of Buddhist figures
Transmission	A formal reading of religious material from teacher to student that authorizes the student to engage in that particular type of meditation
Tsampa	Roasted barley flour, a staple food for Tibetans
Tsok	An offering ceremony, also called Ganachakra Puja
Vajrayana	see Tantrayana
Yogini	Female meditation master

Transliteration Note

Those Tibetan and Sanskrit terms which have not been translated into English have been rendered into a close phonetic equivalent by the translators. The vowel in the word 'Chöd' is pronounced by saying "ee" while making your mouth into an O.

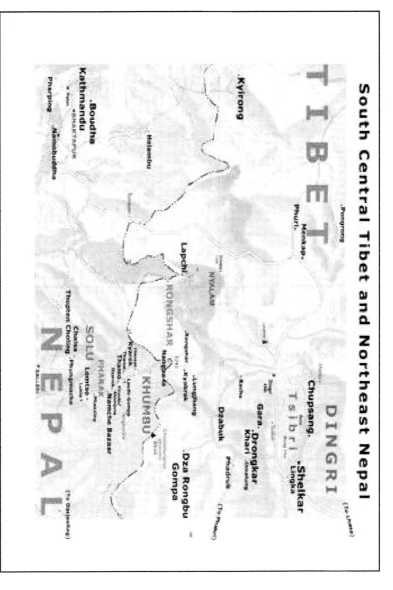

Map of Southern Tibet courtesy of Michael Smith

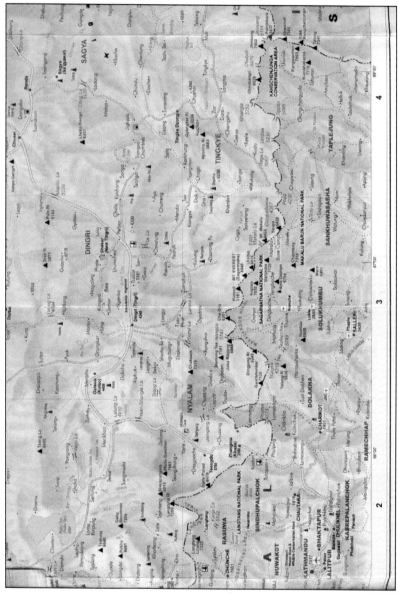

Gondoni, Paulo. Tibet South Central: Road Map. (Kathmandu: Himalaya Map House)

Ruins of the Shelkar Chöde e administration building above the partially rebuilt Shelkar Chöde Monastery.

Above Shelkar Chöde, the ruins of Kari Lama's retreat house

Nyelam, the area through which Lama Wangdu traveled from Tibet to Nepal

Tsipri Mountain, the Holy Mountains near Lama Wangu's birthplace

To give oneself, body, speech, and mind, to the cause of Truth,

Is the best and highest occupation, O Ye Tingri folk.

If ye fail to grasp the meaning, [to the Guru] make ye prayer;

Doubt ye not that understanding will then come, O Tingri folk.

-Padampa Sangye, 10th century

Birth and Early Years

I was born in a village called Palkiri, in the Langkor Valley, which is in the middle of the west Tingri region in Tibet. This region is ringed with holy sites. In the south looms Mt. Everest and in the west stands Lapchi. Behind Tingri is Tsipri. To the northwest is Pongrong and to the north lies Butra.

Tingri itself is a sacred area, the origin of which was prophesied by Shakyamuni Buddha long ago. While the Buddha was teaching the Perfection of Wisdom at Vulture's Peak near Rajgir, India, his disciple Rabjor asked, "Earlier you were teaching us the Perfection of Patience, Effort and the other Perfections. Why, Buddha, are you now teaching only this Perfection of Wisdom?"

The Buddha replied, "Of all the Perfections, this teaching is the most important."

"If it is so precious, to where will it spread in the future?" asked the disciples.

"My teaching will spread from Vulture's Peak to a northern land," answered the Buddha, "and then once again to the north of that.."

Rabjor then asked, "You will pass away and I also will pass away; who then will teach this Perfection of Wisdom in the regions to the north?"

The Buddha prophesied, "In the northern land, my teaching of the Perfection of Wisdom will be spread by my younger sister Kangye Lhamo, and by my disciple Mipham Gonpo. These two will spread the Dharma in the north." (Buddha's sister Kangye Lhamo later became Machik Lapdron.)

When Buddha uttered this, his sister did not reply, but his disciple Mipham Gonpo spoke. "If we two are supposed to spread the Dharma in Tibet, where exactly is the place where we are supposed to teach?"

In reply, the Buddha picked up a stone about the size of a fist and squeezed it, leaving his finger imprints in this rock as if it were butter. "Wherever this stone lands, there you will preach the Perfection of Wisdom in the future and spread my Dharma."

During those days, Tingri was still a lake. When Buddha threw the stone, it fell into this lake, producing the sound "'ding," which reverberated off the surrounding mountains. It is from this sound that the name "Tingri" came to be. After the Buddha passed into Parinirvana, the lake eventually dried up, and people began to inhabit the area.

As prophesied, Mipham Gonpo was later reborn in India as Padampa Sangye, a great Mahasiddha. Mahasiddhas are great beings who appeared several hundred years after Buddha's time; they achieved full enlightenment by following the sacred path of the Mahayana and Tantrayana.

They practiced in forests and lived as wanderers. But these great sages would meet together once each year, in south Palkiri in the Palki Mountains, where they reported their miracles and accomplishments before the Mahasiddha Nagarjuna and Saraha. While the others reported their powers, Dampa Sangye remained silent. Saraha finally asked him, "What about your practice?"

"I do not engage in any practice of enlightenment, in which you go to a Pure Land," replied Dampa, "nor do I want the practices of a lama who sits on a high throne. I want a Dharma that immediately ends the suffering of sentient beings. This is what I am practicing."

"Your practice is truly great," replied Saraha. "This kind of love and compassion is indeed the root to resolving the suffering of sentient beings. Your practice is like the musk of a deer. There are many animals, but the deer is indeed meaningful, because its musk is medicinal and cures many ailments."

Nagarjuna also praised Dampa Sangye's practice. "Your Dharma expels suffering within one moment," Nagarjuna said. "I will call it Pacification – Shije."

While Padampa Sangye was on pilgrimage around Tsipri, he saw Tingri from the top of the mountain; it was covered by snow and appeared below like a pot of white milk. However, he noticed a dark patch of ground in the west, free from any snow, in the shape of an elephant sleeping. (Today that place is called Langkor, the Elephant Valley.) Padampa Sangye traveled down the mountain to see whether he could find the renowned stone the Buddha had thrown in his previous life. When Dampa Sangye came to a certain riverbank, he saw a spot where six musk deer were circumambulating and making mandala offerings. The elephant-shaped patch of ground was the mountain, and Dorje Palmo was the dark place on the ground underneath. The Buddha's stone had landed at the heart of Dorje Palmo.

As Dampa Sangye approached, the six deer – one doe and five fawns – all dissolved into one, and then the group of them dissolved into that very stone thrown from Vulture's Peak so long ago. In this way, Dampa Sangye recovered the stone. For this reason, the place was first called La Kor, "La" meaning "musk deer" and "kor" meaning "to circle." It was here that Padampa established his monastery.

There is yet another version of how Langkor received its name. When Dampa Sangye later established a monastery there and was giving teachings, the king of Porong offered him a white ox without even a single black hair on it. This ox delivered water to a hundred meditators, door to door, in the summertime. In the winter it delivered ice. After finishing its work, the ox would return to Dampa Sangye's monastery and circumambulate it. "Lang" means "ox" and "Kor" means "to circle," so the area came to be named Langkor. It is thus correct to say either Lakor or Langkor. It was in this place that I was born.

My Parents

Although she came from a wealthy household in Langkor, my mother worked as a maid for my father's family. She was the second of three children, all girls. She was not considered especially attractive, and some even called her "pig face." My father was the eldest of seven brothers and was the wealthiest man in Penak village in Tingri. His family was named Penakpa, but people called him Topgye. The youngest brother in the family was a monk at Shelka Chöde monastery, which housed about three hundred monks.

While working as a maid for the Penakpa family, my mother became pregnant with me through secret relations with my father, Topgye. His legal wife, whose family was from Ling-Shar in the north (near Tsipri), did not have any children herself. Their family name was Chuponda.

This wife had a brother who often stayed with the Penakpa family. He also claimed to be my father, and so basically, I had two fathers. One was the son of the Penak family and the other was his brother-in-law. Both were sleeping with my mother, the maidservant, so both claimed to be my father.

When my mother became pregnant, she stopped working and went back to her own family in Langkor. Neither of my two fathers really took care of her during the pregnancy; it was her sisters who cared for her and acted as midwives during childbirth.

There was a lineage of direct descendants of Pa Gya Gompa in Langkor. Pa Gya Gompa was at the time a great practitioner of Dampa Sangye, and his spiritual lineage still existed in a family with one lay practitioner and one monk. From a Dharma family lineage point of view, this family was very sacred. My mother used to address them both as "Uncle," although I don't know if this was out of politeness or if they were actually related.

Just before my birth, my mother started bleeding heavily as if it were her menstrual period. She asked her sister to go to her uncle for a divination. He gave this prediction: "Before a woman gives birth to a son, she will get bleeding called 'first blood.' You do not need to worry; she will soon give birth to a son. She will not have a miscarriage."

Birth

The early morning sun poured through the window of the small room where I was born. It was the tenth day of the first month of the Tibetan lunar calendar in 1936. The lamas were performing ceremonial offerings in the monastery nearby, as is the custom on the tenth day of each lunar month. My birth was uneventful, except that I was born wrapped in a pocket of membrane – the amniotic sac. My mother remarked with shock that I looked "like a bubble." Indeed, both my mother and my aunts were afraid to touch me, as I did not look like a human being!

They called for an old village woman. "If something is born like this," she told them, "and if it's a boy, then this is good. It needs to be opened up." So the old woman opened up this "bubble" and there I was. However, when I was released from the membrane, the umbilical cord was wrapped around me like a meditation belt, and I was crying. The old woman advised, "It is a very auspicious sign that your son was born with his cord wrapped around him like this. Since he doesn't really have a father, you should take special care of him."

Then my mother sent my aunt to the lama for a name. When she arrived at the lama's house, the lamas were practicing Chöd from Padampa's Shije lineage. At the moment she arrived, they were reciting the part of the Chöd text regarding the practice of "Wangdu," meaning to subjugate and overpower obstacles. "A son was born with the umbilical cord around his neck like a meditation belt," explained my aunt, nearly out of breath. "Will you please give him a name?"

In accordance with what the lama was reading at the time of her arrival, he said, "His name will be Tsering Wangdu." Thus I received this auspicious name, which means "One of Long Life who Subjugates."

Early Experiences

When I was growing up, natural scars ran in lines all over my body. Some people said, "Your body has the design of a tiger," while others said, "It is like leaves," or "It is like scars."

When I was just beginning to talk, one night I woke my mother. "Don't lie down," I said to her. "Get up; we should pray."

My mother replied, "I don't know what prayer I should say."

So I told her, "OM AMI DEWA HRIH, Dewa chen du kye war shog," which means "May I be born in the Pureland of Bliss."

"OM AMI DEWA HRIH" is the mantra of Buddha Amitabha. This is the prayer my mother said I taught her when I was first able to speak.

When I was old enough to walk and run, I didn't play like the other children my age who played a lot of games. Instead, I made stupas with small stones and did many prostrations to them. Two representatives of the Langkor village arrived one day from the central government in Lhasa. The official and his wife walked around our fields. They watched me doing prostrations and thought I must be an incarnation of a lama who had been very devoted in practice. I remember they were kind to me and gave me many sweets.

Even when I was small, I would give Dharma teachings to the five or six boys and girls who played with me. The children would come with tsampa (roasted barley flour) used to make grain cakes. But instead of making cakes we made ceremonial offerings for rituals.

They soon gave me the nickname "little lama." When other children harassed the village chickens and broke their eggs, I cried and told them not to act in that way. After that, whenever I was around, they refrained from killing animals or breaking eggs. Among my friends to whom I taught Dharma was a girl who could not hear well. We used to play games in which I took her on my lap and told her Dharma stories in her ear so she could understand.

But my young life was about to change. There was a family called Ugyen Shika in the north of Tingri who were related to my family, they had no male child. Ugyen Shika's adult son wanted to take my mother to his family, and he also wanted to take me along. When the Penak family heard this, they confiscated me from my mother, separating mother and son.

The fourteenth day of the sixth month of the Tibetan calendar is the anniversary of the Parinirvana of Padampa Sangye, called the Langkor Religious Feast. This festival is based on the events that occurred after Padampa died. When the villagers and devoted students expressed their grief and sorrow at the time Dampa Sangye died, he woke from the dead and told them all, "Don't cry over me; rather, on this day of Religious Feast, you should dance, sing and offer prayers."

So on that day all of Tingri would come together to join in the festivities. And that year at the festival, the people sang in commentary, "It's a custom to stop the foal from drinking milk from the mare, and it is the custom of Penakpa to stop the baby from drinking its mother's milk." They were referring to how the Penakpa family took me away from my mother while I was still being breast fed.

Growing Pains

Thus I stayed with my father Topgye and his legal wife. I also lived for a time with my uncle Norbu Thondrup, who shared the same wife as my father. Polyandry was a common practice in Tibet at the time. Because they were otherwise childless, they brought me up with great love. The Penakpa family was wealthy, and so there was a large community of people living in the household, including grandmothers, grandfathers and so forth, about eighteen members in total. So for a few years during this time I was very well cared for.

I clearly remember my grandmother's death, which was closely followed by the death of my father's legal wife. These two women had taken special care in raising me. After their deaths, the Penakpa family got a new wife, but as it turned out, she did not care much for me at all. In fact, she would send me out to look after the flocks of sheep in the fields rather than have me around the home.

Five or six other children would come with me when I grazed the sheep. I stayed within the stone wall that surrounded our field, and using rocks from the wall, I would make small stupas. Carrying a tiny ritual drum and bell in my shepherd bag, I did religious practice in the pastures. I have been told that when I was small, I was like a yogi and didn't like to wear many clothes. At our home, the ground floor was where they kept the sheep. I lived on the middle floor, and I turned my room into a shrine area with an altar, using small mud statues and apricot pits as offerings, even making tiny clothes for the statues out of old candy wrappers.

Because my family kept flocks of sheep, there was a regular schedule when animals would be taken to slaughter. My parents would select a sheep to be killed, and I was required to hold the sheep down on the block. At first, I cried pitifully and begged that the sheep not be killed. Later, I refused to allow the sheep to be butchered. My parents had to select a sheep and hide it from me before I woke up. On the day they killed the sheep, I would not laugh or smile. My parents said, "Lama is angry, his face is darkened," and they called me "Black-faced lama." I was about eight or nine at the time.

In the fall we would harvest the barley and move it to the pastures to separate the grain from the stalks. I would sleep in the grain fields at night, and during the day I would graze the sheep. I remember that whenever the villagers lost their yaks or sheep or other animals, they would come to me and ask for a divination. Although I didn't have the proper beads or dice for this, I would say, "Go to such and such a place to find your animal." And almost always they would indeed find it there. Other children would also ask me to dispel rain and hail, but this worked only some of the time!

When I was a child, I rarely ate meat. During one spring, the water went bad. Because I was eating just tsampa, I lacked nutrition; my body, feet and head became swollen and yellow. My father, Topgye, was worried that I would die if I didn't eat some meat. He boiled some meat, rice and milk into a soup and gave it to me. Rice was very rare at the time; after eating this hearty soup for a few days, the swelling disappeared and I was cured.

Later, my new stepmother gave birth to two daughters, and she became even more jealous of and cruel to me. "Your mother is in Langkor and your father is in north Tingri," she said. "Why are you still staying here?" She was so mean to me, especially after the new children were born. Living in this manner, there was no one to teach me basic skills in reading or writing, let alone Dharma.

One day in the autumn while looking after the grains, I was dozing off and heard some people talking. I looked up to see that a lama named Ugyen had come to the field to teach his son how to read a text. Each day I would watch him, and listen, and then repeat to myself the same things at night. One night, when I recited the alphabet, my father was surprised.

"How did you learn how to pronounce the alphabet?" he asked.

"Mr. Ugyen is teaching his son and I learned from him," I replied.

My father thought, "Well, I certainly should teach my son, too." He managed to find a text on the alphabet and gave this to me. I was able to easily learn everything in one day.

Where I lived in Tibet, we would go once or twice a year to the watermill to grind barley. Mr. Ugyen was the man in charge of the watermill, and I would go there to help for five or six days. When the simple beggars and the ascetic practitioners (who relied on alms to eat) heard that I was working at the watermill, they all came, knowing that I would give them grain. There were also many fish in the river next to the watermill. Sometimes I also made ritual offerings from grains, did practice, and threw the offerings into the water to feed the fishes.

In the fall when people were harvesting, yogis and meditators would come to beg for alms. I would go around with them for two or three days and then return home. That is why the yogis and meditators who sought alms all loved me and thought well of me.

Meeting the Guru

When still quite young I told my uncle, who was a monk at Shelkar Chöde monastery, that I was prepared to enter a life of Dharma, and I kept a bag with a ritual drum and bell ready to leave at a moment's notice. But still they did not send me to the monastery to study. However, one day my family invited the great Trülshik Rinpoche to consecrate a shrine room in the house.

Rinpoche saw my own shrine room and playthings, and he asked my father what this was. My father replied, "It's just my son playing." Trülshik Rinpoche was pleased, though, and he said, "This boy must be the reincarnation of a Dharma practitioner. He should be sent to a monastery to study." He asked me whether I would like to come to his monastery or to Shelkar Chöde monastery.

"I'm not going to either monastery," I replied. "I'm going to practice Dharma on my own."

At hearing this, Trülshik Rinpoche became silent. He went away. Later, my father told me that if I had said I wanted to go to Trülshik Rinpoche's monastery, he would have taken care of me. But because I refused to go to any monastery whatsoever, I was not taken anywhere.

"You do not have good fortune," he told me, "or you could have been completely cared for by Trülshik Rinpoche."

Another time, my mother asked Tsa Rungbu Sangye, a high lama from Trülshik Rinpoche's monastery, about the circumstances of my birth and about the scars on my body. "He is a reincarnation of a practitioner," said the high lama. "One day someone will come to take him. When that time comes, don't feel any doubt, and just give him to that person." Upon seeing the markings on my body, he suggested that they change my name to Ugyen Dorje Punstok.

Shortly thereafter, I developed terrible pains in my knees and legs. My family had a special guru from Kham (Eastern Tibet) named Naptra Rinpoche, whom they considered their main lama. He was well respected by everyone in the village, and so I was put on a horse, held up between two large sacks of grain with a board strapped on top like a bed, so they could take me to him to discover whether he could help me. They laid me on this wooden plank and roped me to the horse, lying down, because I couldn't sit up without pain.

At the moment of my arrival, Naptra Rinpoche was conducting a ceremony on the rooftop of a newly completed building, and the monks began blowing the long, deep-sounding horns – the sang dung. The sound frightened my horse, causing it to bolt in fear and throw me off. My father and the servant Dolkar were terrified that I had broken something or further damaged my legs. But when I fell from the horse, I landed on a pile of sheep droppings without injury or pain. I was just standing in a pile of sheep dung!

After that I was cleaned up and taken to see Naptra Rinpoche. "This boy should practice Dharma and take vows; he will then have a long life," said Rinpoche. "Otherwise his life will be short." He said I would be a good practitioner.

Upon hearing and understanding this, my parents asked the lama to take care of my teaching; they asked him to take a lock of my hair, so that he would be my root lama, or main teacher. Rinpoche asked me if I would like to practice Dharma. I said yes. So he cut a lock of my hair and gave me the spiritual name Ngawang Chösang. I remained, along with my parents, at the monastery for fifteen days. When I first arrived, I had been sick with the pain in my knees and legs. But after spending two weeks with Rinpoche, I recovered from all my ailments and no longer had any pain.

Further Studies

I was twelve years old when I began my next two years at Naptra monastery. I learned many practices from Naptra Rinpoche. I received instructions on the subtle energies in our bodies for the ejection of our consciousness, along with other meditations and explanations. After two years my father said, "Now you are a good Dharma practitioner; it's time for you to learn more advanced reading and writing." So he took me to my uncle at the Shelkar Chöde monastery. I was fourteen years old when I walked to the Shelkar monastery with just my small shepherd bag.

At that time, my uncle Pönlop Champa was the spiritual head of the monastery. I arrived at my uncle's house just as the sun was rising. He was happy to see me, calling me by my old nickname "Child Deprived of Milk." He offered me sweet cookies. During my stay, my uncle taught me how to read, write and spell. He also taught me the Manjushri mantra, so that I would develop a strong and penetrating intellect. Every morning I arose to recite prayers in front of him. In the daytime after the daily ceremonies, eight or nine monks would come to learn dialectics from him. I would serve them tea and listen in. When the monks sometimes forgot what was taught, I was able to remember and remind them. Perhaps the Manjushri mantra had given me a good memory!

There were many wall paintings in the monastery, and I would spend hours and hours looking at them. I noticed that there weren't any images of Guru Rinpoche. There was, however, a small statue of Guru Rinpoche on top of the Mani wall at the gate to the stupa, and whenever I passed by it on the way to my classes, I would stop and stare at it. Also, in the main hall of the monastery, there was a painting of Dampa Sangye and Milarepa meeting and competing in miracles. Sometimes I would go there just to stare at that painting and study it for long periods of time.

At Shelkar Chöde, according to tradition, a high lama comes from Sera Monastery in Lhasa to serve as a Khenpo, or dialectics teacher. One year, a certain Khenpo got to know me and said, "This boy is very intelligent and adorable." He liked me very much, and he offered me cookies and fruits. This scholarly lama then asked me if I would like to be a monk at his monastery.

"No, I don't want to become a monk," I replied. "I would instead like to be a yogi and stay away from monasteries. I would like to practice by myself."

The Khenpo protested. "What's the use of becoming a yogi without first becoming a monk?"

"I would be of no benefit to the Dharma if I became a monk," I replied. "I could benefit the Dharma and all sentient beings only as a yogi, through deep meditation and practice on my own."

Return to the Lama

After I had learned how to read and write well, I became homesick for Tingri and my village. So at age fifteen I made the journey home, accompanied by my father. It must have been spring when we made this journey home, because we had to cross the swollen Bumchu River. The winter's snow and ice were melting, and the river was full and fast and overflowing, with great ice blocks heaving down the stream. This made for a very dangerous crossing indeed. My father asked me to recite mantras while we crossed the river, so we wouldn't be hit and knocked over by these great chunks of lurching ice. This I did, and we managed to cross the river safely.

By this time, I was fifteen years old, and I had grown apart from my real mother and her family. There was no one any more that I felt close to in my heart. When I stayed at my father's house, his new wife was jealous of me, and she would tell me to leave. I argued with her all the time. It was just my father and uncle and grandfather who really cared for me. They would always respectfully offer me the best place to sit, and otherwise express their respect and concern.

After my stay in Tingri, I was sent to the Naptra monastery to again study with my lama. I stayed in a monk's room near the courtyard. At the time, there were nuns living in the monastery, one who was from Pongrong in the west, and another nun from the north. They both asked to marry me, but I told them it was not appropriate for me to marry at that time, and I didn't become intimate with either of them.

During my stay there, I received all the teachings on mandala offerings, Vajrasattva practice and other preliminary practices. That year I offered 100,000 prostrations and 100,000 mandala offerings, recited 100,000 hundred-syllable mantras, and performed 1,200,000 Guru Rinpoche mantras. I was now sixteen years old, and ready to be initiated into more advanced meditation practices.

Political Intrigue in Feudal Tibet

I returned home from the monastery when I was seventeen years old. Among the family duties that my father then asked me to assume was looking after our sheep as they grazed.

One day as I brought the sheep down to the river as usual, I came upon a man in a white chuba, his white horse drinking deeply from the clear water at river's edge. He asked me, "Are you the one called Tsering Wangdu?" I nodded my head in the affirmative. He told me that my uncle, who normally stayed at Shelkar Chöde monastery, had been appointed as an official of Thong-Mön Shika village, a hamlet within the small county of Thong-Mön. The gentleman in white, Kisong Thundrup, had been sent all this way to fetch me, and he insisted that we leave for the village the next day. But I refused, explaining to him that I would have to go to Naptra monastery first to seek the blessing of my lama.

I went to our house, and my father explained that my uncle was now the main official of Thong-mön County. "This is a very high position," he said, "so he needs some assistance. Furthermore, he is not in good health, so your help is required immediately. You should indeed leave tomorrow – pack your damaru and bell."

The next morning I mounted my own horse and left with Kisong Thundrup, crossing Tingri pass. That night we reached Phatruk Gara village, and in two more days we reached a village called Gang-gya. The name relates to the great fertility of this area, for Gang means "one" and gya means "hundred." It was said that for every one seed of grain planted in this rich valley, one hundred sprouts would grow! The grain and general storage for the Thong-Mön Shika administration was located here at Gang-gya.

When I arrived, there was much drinking and dancing going on, and the family that hosted me treated me very well, according to the best of local customs, offering me meat and rice beer. They had a pair of beautiful daughters; the elder was named Ugyen Dolma, and the younger was called Kalsang Dolma. I was to meet them again in a few years. The next day, as we were leaving on horseback, they kindly offered me a flask of rice beer for the journey.

The Villages

We eventually arrived at Thong-Mön proper. Thong-Mön means "the moment it is seen, it is liked," an expression that connotes something calm, peaceful and rich. Appropriately, the official's residence in Thong-Mön village was a beautiful five-story building surrounded by many beautiful trees. In the middle of the entrance gate was a large prayer wheel.

When we arrived, a young man was standing in front of the wheel without any clothes at all – completely naked. "Who is this man?" I asked.

"He has no father," replied Kisong. "His mother is very poor. He simply has no clothes to wear."

A feeling of great compassion arose in me, and the next day I invited him to my room and offered him both food and clothing. I made him my attendant, and from then on he accompanied me wherever I went. His name was Migmar. My uncle, whose official title was Dewa Shika, was living in a large room within the main residence. He told me that I had been appointed to take full charge of his affairs of state, and that I must also attend to the farms and properties. I learned that I would stay at this post for at least two years, and that I could not go to the monastery for further religious study until I had finished my assignment here. As it turned out, I would remain there for a full three years.

A village official briefed me on accessing the grain store, the rules for distributing grains, and the procedures for making records of loans. I learned where to keep the rice beer, the grasses, and the roasted flour. I quickly learned that although the official's residence was very rich and formidable, the villagers themselves were very poor. Only a few were reasonably comfortable, while the others had to borrow both grain for their sustenance and grass to feed their livestock.

There were many rooms in the Thong-Mön Shika residence. The sheep and various other goods were kept on the ground floor. The storage areas for the meat, rice beer, roasted flour, and many other items were on the next floor. On the third floor were the official residence and shrine rooms, while the fourth floor housed the emergency grains stored in case of famine. Many of these relief supplies had been there for years, sealed in by mud bricks. On the uppermost floor were rooms dedicated to the male and female protector deities such as Palden Lhamo and Damchen Dorje Lekpa. It was in one of these shrine rooms that the annual ritual offerings ceremony was held. The main sacred object there was a foot-high statue of Palden Lhamo riding a mule. For persons engaged in business affairs, this protector is able to confer a great deal of success and profit.

The residence quarters themselves also contained many valuable objects and luxurious furnishings.

The villages of Samdrup Khang, Kang Sar, and Lha-zuk were also part of the Thong-Mön district. In the north were Gang-gya and Tza-kor. Kar-da, Trak, and Bum-Thang villages were in the east, Chu-shar and Yön-Che were in the south, and on the other side of a mountain pass were Lha-par, Gadong, Tey, Yejang, and Tsogo villages. Besides our residence, Tsogo village was the other area where the Shika administration stored grains. All of these places were under the jurisdiction of the Thong-Mön administration, and people came from these many small surrounding villages to work here. They were paid with roasted flour, tea, raw barley, or rice beer. In turn, each group of ten workers had to provide their own single pot to be filled with rice beer during the day.

If the workers were paid strictly in accordance with this regulation, it would barely provide them with enough to survive. So I did not follow the prescribed rules, but instead gave them as much as possible. If I was supposed to give one clay pot of rice beer, I gave two.

Sometimes villagers came to the courtyard and waited in the hot sun. When the housekeepers told me of this, I gave the poorest people oil, clothes, and roasted flour. After some time, poor people heard about such things, and they would travel long distances to receive this charity.

Just below, in Kharta village, lived a group of people who had once been wealthy but had fallen into extreme poverty. Oddly, they retained the surnames of the upper class. Previously their houses had been large, but now they were crumbling heaps. They didn't have enough to eat, and survived mainly on thin vegetable soup. The Shika administration had records of grain loans made to these people from many years before, amounting to some 10,000 measures. Although this debt was clearly documented, there was no hope of ever recovering the grain from these destitute people.

On my visit to Kharta village, I told the family to bring a yak horn full of grain as a symbol of repaying all the old debts. After they had made this symbolic gesture, I simply burned the old loan documents. "Now, you should no longer worry about these old loans to the Shika administration," I told them. "You should feel as though you have paid them back with this yak horn of grain. However, from now on, whatever new grains you borrow from me, you must pay back the following year."

Prior to my arrival, Shika village had no tradition of Buddhist priests performing ritual offerings or ceremonies. I decided to invite a holy Nyingma lama from a nearby village. I asked him to perform an empowerment and a ritual feast offering for everyone. After the rituals, we distributed food to all the families in attendance. For his services I offered the lama appropriate donations and then sent him back to his own village. Later, I also invited a high Kagyu lama named Gyaltsen, who lived on the northeast side in Tsogo village. He wore the long dreadlocks of a yogi, a non-monastic lama who never cut his hair and lived as an ascetic. He gave empowerments and food offerings in the village, which were then distributed to all in attendance.

After two years at Thong-Mön, I came to know everything that went on in the villages of my jurisdiction. I told any family taking loans that whatever grains they would take now, they must pay back next fall with interest. "When you need grain again next year, and you have proven yourselves responsible, I will give them to you regardless of debts incurred before my arrival." I told this to the poor families who usually borrowed only small amounts so that they would not have large loans to pay back.

I told the wealthy families the same thing. These rich villagers often invited me to perform ceremonies. I would stay with them for two or three days, performing rituals as well as enjoying myself. I soon earned the nickname "New Shika Wangdu-la." Before my assignment as supervisor began, if a Shika official approached, the villagers would become terrified and run away. Now when I arrived, no one was scared. On the contrary, everyone came to meet me, drink and dance, and have a good time. I also offered barley, meat, and roasted flour to the Dharma practitioners every year. Still, sometimes I had to go out to talk with people who had not repaid their loans. And so in this way it continued for three years.

In the fall of my second year, at age eighteen, I happened to stay in Gang-gya village where Shika's grain was stored. This was the place where I had stopped on my earlier journey to the administration job, where two beautiful girls had offered me rice beer as I left there on my horse. Earlier, in the spring, when the villagers were busy planting, I had given this family seeds to plant. Later that fall, during the harvest time when the grains were gathered, I went down to collect the crops.

Growing up in a small Tingri village, I had hardly associated with girls. In fact, when I was small, I mostly practiced Dharma and kept to myself. But at seventeen, I had been appointed as the Shika official and now was staying with these kind people. That was when I first really noticed the two daughters. That fall, I spent time with the younger daughter, whose name was Kalsang Drolma, and it was not long before we decided to marry.

Kalsang Drolma was beautiful, and she had a kind heart. She was a wonderful singer and I enjoyed listening to her voice. We were married after only a short time.

For our wedding, we went to visit a very special mountain in Gang-gya with a cave; behind the mountain is a tall stone that looks like the Buddha. From the front, this mountain looks like Vajrayogini, and a large river flows across at its feet. In front of the river is a rock with a bowl-like impression. Here golden water flows out; it is considered blessing water from the dakinis. Just by this rock is a large cave, large enough that twelve people can fit inside. Many people came to celebrate our wedding, and there was a lot of dancing. This was where we spent our honeymoon after everyone left.

After our wedding, Kalsang Drolma returned with me to Shika for a short time, then she went back to stay in her own village while I worked. Because I was a Nyingma practitioner, I taught her some practices, and I taught her to read and write. In the summertime, I worked in the Shika office taking care of the grain storage while she stayed with her parents. In the fall, after the harvest, my wife and I would go to Tingri to see Naptra Rinpoche and receive teachings from him.

There was another grain store of Thong-Mön in a place called Yechang. At this place, I had another wife named Nyama Tronma. Being so far apart, these wives had no knowledge of each other. It took three days on foot to travel from one wife's village to that of the other, and even the dialects were a little different. Both wives, however, were very virtuous. Nyama Tronma did not bear any children. Kalsang Drolma had a son, but he died after three days and it was a year before she had a child again.

The Conspiracy

While I was an official in Shika, one of the residents had a dispute with my family. His main residence was in Gang-gya, but he also had property in other areas. He was a wealthy man and was friendly with other officials; he often prevailed in any disputes that arose.

Over the years, this man acquired or took over lands from other people. He eventually became obsessed with overseeing his houses and his lands. One year he seized some land from behind our house, and the case was taken to court. He and his allies wanted the power that was granted to Shika officials, and he suspected that I would use my power to become wealthy and influential. Of course this would threaten the legal case against him, and so he hatched a plan.

He asked people in the area about me, and about the Thong-Mön Shika.

And these are some of the things he heard:

"The Thong-Mön Shika official himself is sick and staying in a monastery. One of his relatives, someone named Wangdu, is working in the office. This Wangdu is inviting Nyingma and Kagyu lamas and distributing riches to them."

"We received an officer who is a spiritual administrator and we are very happy with him."

"He gives to people as much as they can carry. People come from faraway places."

"He broke down all the rigid rules of the old administration."

"This lama brought many holy objects to the village."

"High officials are supposed to live in the official residence and take care of the administration, but this Wangdu goes to everyone's homes, even those of the poor people. He doesn't just sit on his high seat."

Normally the officials check on the size of the harvest when the grains are separated. But during my time there, I stopped checking the harvest. I simply told people, "As long as you repay your loans to me, I don't need to assess your crops."

The people thus told the wealthy businessman, "Thong-Mön inhabitants had to eat in hiding before, but since Wangdu came, we don't need to hide any more. We can have fun and enjoy ourselves. We are very happy."

Stories and rumors such as these were spread throughout the area. The Shelkar monastery, which was Gelugpa and had political authority over all administrations, also heard these things.

At that time, a lama named Chesa was the most important monk in Shelkar monastery; he led some three hundred monks. The wealthy businessman reported to the lama Chesa that I gave grains to all the practitioners, and that the Shika storage was now empty. The Shelkar monastery received its grains from the Shika storehouse, which I was in charge of. Thus, when the head lama got this news, he recounted the proverb, "You eat the grass in the pasture but defecate in the cliffs." In other words, the efforts put into the village administration were not profitable for them.

This man's wife had a relative who was a monk at a monastery. The next step in their plan was to offer this monk the opportunity to take over the Shika administration. They persuaded him that doing so would be very beneficial for everyone.

So this monk reported to Chesa, the high lama of the Shelkar Chöde monastery, saying, "The real Shika official staying in this monastery is sick. His relative who is working in Thong-Mön is a lay practitioner, giving everything away and not taking care of taxes. He is offering everything in ritual feasts and giving alms to beggars. Because of this, there is no hope of getting any grains for the Shelkar monastery. If you don't replace him, the Thong-Mön Shika storehouses will be empty!"

It turned out that the high lama was also from the Tsedru Meta village in Patruk, so they became close friends and forged an alliance – they became of one heart. The wife's monk relative told the head lama that I should resign from the Thong-Mön administration. His excuse was that I had invited Nyingma and Kagyu lamas to do pujas, and that I was giving everything away as ritual feast offerings. This monk made a secret deal with the head lama, saying, "If you make the Shika resign and give me his position, I will give you and your entourage food for three years, along with whatever else you need for your house."

Normally this high lama was a spiritual person, but he succumbed to the manipulation and the promise of wealth. With such a mind he promised his co-conspirators, "I will make the current Shika resign and will give you the post. In return you must give me grains and other things I desire." Thus an agreement was made.

Stepping Down

My uncle's roommate was a monk called Pönlop Champa, the highest spiritual lama at the monastery. He was the one who gave teachings, performed the hair-cutting ceremony, and taught dialectics. He was actively involved in spiritual practices and did not take part in any worldly affairs. Even compared with the other monks, he was poor and lived austerely. He was a real practitioner and never conducted any secular activities in the monastery. Pönlop Champa was, in essence, the spiritual director and the high lama, while Chesa (who had formed this unethical alliance) was the political director of the monastery.

One day the political director called for the roommate Pönlop Champa and told him, "I have heard that because of your roommate's illness and your focus on spiritual practice, there is now a young man called Wangdu working in the Thong-Mön administration. He is giving everything away to beggars and practitioners. The people are saying they are happy, that they have a spiritual administrator, and yet he is giving everything away. We need to change this state of affairs. You should make preparations immediately to transfer the administration duties to someone else."

Pönlop calmly responded to this. "We did not ask to be appointed as high officials of Thong-Mön. You appointed us – and you appointed a sick man to act as an official! I am busy teaching dialectics and practicing meditation; I don't have time to look after the administration. We sent for this young man because there was no one else able or willing to do the work. We are practitioners of Dharma, and you appointed us against our will. Why don't you just take this responsibility back?!"

These two lamas had no need to quarrel at all, but with these simple words it was decided to hand over the administration to someone else. The high lama said to Pönlop Champa, "You should go to Thong-Mön Shika administration building for one month to prepare to transfer everything. When you are ready, send me a message, and I will send down a new administrator."

The Pönlop came to the monks' quarters with a few others to help prepare for the takeover. "Our time is finished," he told me, "and within one month we must hand this over to another official. We must make the entire bookkeeping clear. We need to account for the number of sheep and animals in stock."

And so I began preparations. I took inventory and made records of all the existing grains. Whatever was loaned out, I recorded. When all the preparations were complete, I told the Pönlop that we were ready to proceed and that he should send for the new official.

Meanwhile, the head monk of Shelkar approached the protector deity and performed a divination in order to choose the new official. He claimed he had a vision of the monk from the businessman's wife's family, but as we know, they had previously made a deal. This new monk soon arrived with an entourage of other monks to take over our office.

Open Conflict

I handed over everything to him. At first it all worked out well, but later this monk made allegations that things were not as they should be, and that there were some improprieties. Specifically, he complained of two things that were not in order.

"Firstly, this Wangdu Shika gave feast offerings with Nyingma and Kagyu lamas. Gelugpa lamas have no history of giving offerings to Nyingma and Kagyu lamas. We Gelugpas are masters of the government. We should not even offer a little bit of the sound of a bell or a waft of incense to a Nyingma lama. But this Wangdu welcomed Nyingma and Kagyu lamas with musical instruments, and even had them give empowerments and rituals to the people. All this is simply not permitted."

Pönlop Champa, who was also of the Gelugpa order, retorted, "Although the offerings were made by Nyingma and Kagyu lamas, the food was eaten by the people of the village. Just as there is nothing wrong with saying Om Mani Padme Hum, this is just spiritual practice, and all the people received benefit. Only you are to blame for creating a problem!"

"Secondly," continued the monk, "this Wangdu has burned all the historical loan documents of the Kharta valley. If these documents are not restored, I will not take over the office." The new officer had already given back the yak horn full of grain to the families in the Kharta valley.

"Take back your yak horn worth of grain," he had told them. "It means nothing. We need to make a new agreement."

The families were still very poor and they still got by on watered-down soup. "We offered these yak horns to Wangdu-la," they had told him. "If you don't like this, give them back. If you want to make a new arrangement, do it. If the number is 2,000 you can write 20,000. If the number is 10,000 you can write 100,000. It doesn't really matter! You are looking only at numbers that we are unable to pay back. It is only paper to us, and your paper means nothing! If you ask us to sign it once, we will sign it ten times."

Pönlop and the monk broke into an argument over this, and they disagreed for some time. The monk finally said, "Now we are not in a position to agree, so I think we need a witness."

In Shelkar monastery there was a scholar working as a secretary. The high lama of the monastery sent this scholar to Shika to witness the handover. He investigated the situation at the main residence. "Wangdu-la himself doesn't even have one small possession," the scholar said at a meeting. "Everything he has done has been for the benefit of the people. The other officials have never done this."

And to the new monk he said, "You are a barbarian!"

The new monk stared at the scholar, who continued his lecture. "Pönlop has kindly agreed to hand over the power to you. He is your own lama and teacher in the monastery! If you bring your lama to court, you become a real enemy of your lama and to the dharma. Think what you are doing!"

At this the new monk became even angrier. "You were sent by the head lama to witness this handover! You were not sent here to call me names. Now you call me a barbarian and an enemy of the dharma?!"

"For many years I have been the secretary of the monastery," replied the scholar. "You seem to think that giving alms is a bad thing; I cannot be your witness."

The argument continued like this for some time.

In My Defense

Finally the scholar decided to return to the monastery and report everything back to the abbot, Lama Chesa. "As you know, the new official is very immoral," he said. "He brought his own teacher down to a mundane level. The real Shika is sick and unable to work. The person working for him, Wangdu, has not given anything to the monastery, not even a table. But he has given alms and done other spiritual activities, such as inviting Nyingma or Kagyu lamas to give feast offerings. He doesn't have anything himself, not even a horse to ride on. All he did was burn two or three old loan documents from families who wouldn't possibly have been able to pay the loans back."

He also reprimanded the high lama. "You said your divination told you he would be the right official to take power. You said this in front of the Protector Deity. You didn't need to do such a thing. In the Shelkar monastery there are over three hundred monks with families sponsoring them. Any one of these people could have been sent there. You didn't need to do a divination for such worldly things."

"If this is the case, I will go myself to witness the handover," Chesa finally said. And he came down to the official residence with nine other monks.

But the old monks beseeched him. "Up until now the high officials have never gone down to do such small jobs," they said. "It's inauspicious to leave your seat empty for such a little thing. You could send some other people to see to this." But the high monk did not listen.

Since Pönlop had come to the residence over a month before, problems had escalated to such an extent that two of the highest officials from the monastery became involved. While they were discussing the matter, the high lama asked, "Who is this Wangdu who gave the feast offerings?" He was told, and he called for me.

In the head monk's presence, the new monk official reported everything he had accused me of, including inviting Kagyu and Nyingma lamas, giving feast offerings, and burning the old loan documents.

The head lama asked me solemnly, "Did you do all of that?"

"Yes, I did." I answered. "In the Shika residence there was so much grain, and it was so old and rotten that even the horses wouldn't eat it. The villagers didn't have grain at all, so I gave each person one packet of food from the rituals. I also went to the villages when they asked for loans, in order to see whether the families really did not have enough food to eat. I burned the loan documents for them, because they really will never have enough to pay back these loans."

To my surprise, the head lama did not reprimand me. Instead he told the new administrator monk, "You shouldn't do this! Wangdu has nothing of his own. If you want a meal, put your hand in the flour bag. If there is nothing wrong with the flour, eat it."

The monks of Shelkar decided to investigate me to see if I had been honest. They questioned the villagers about my activities. Some villagers reported, "During the summer he always worked for the Shika. In the winter he always went to lamas and did practice in caves. He has no horse and always traveled on foot." They also checked to see if I had given my wife jewelry, but they learned only that her family was supporting me. Thus the high official developed confidence in me, and he took my side in all this.

Finally the high lama made his decision. "Wangdu hasn't done anything wrong. There is enough grain to feed the monastery, and all the animals are accounted for – nothing is missing. The other Shika officials have just barely fulfilled the requirements and taken what they wanted, while Wangdu has taken nothing for himself. All he did was make some feast offerings and rituals."

The new Shika and the high lama argued for some time, and then the lama concluded the discussion. "You really shouldn't act this way toward Wangdu," he said. "If you refuse to take office, I will simply appoint someone else. You are not obligated to do this job." To me he simply said, "You can go home now; there is no more problem."

Before I left, the monks asked me, "What possessions do you have?"

"I have a damaru, a kangling, some texts, and offering pots," I said. "And, of course, my wife."

Everyone laughed at this. "If you have only these," they told me, "then it is easy for you to leave with nothing to carry."

So I left.

The Epilogue

Sometime after that, Chesa, the political head lama of Shelkar monastery, left the Shika residence and traveled to his home village nearby. He stayed at the hot springs in his village for seven days, and then began his journey back to the monastery. He stopped for a tea break just before reaching Chela, a high mountain pass on the way. The monks arranged tea and food for him there, and the lama asked all the monks to make offerings to the Protector deities before eating.

Just as the monks made the offering prayer, Chesa's cup broke in half, just like that – CRACK! Suddenly he felt very ill. They again poured tea for him, and the lama again asked them to make offering prayers to the Protector deities. But before the tea reached his mouth the second time, he collapsed and died from a stroke.

When the political director passed away, Pönlop had to do the Powa funeral ceremony for him!

It was not necessary for all of this to come to such ends, but such is often the result of such worldly bickering, fighting, and bitter feelings.

Practice and Prophesy:
Journeying 108 Funeral Grounds

After my duties with the Shika office, I was once again able to concentrate on the practice of meditation. I made pilgrimages and undertook many meditation retreats in caves, including the practice known as the fivefold hundred thousand: 100,000 refuge and bodhichitta prayers, 100,000 prostrations, 100,000 mandala offerings, 100,000 Vajrasattva mantras, and 1,200,000 Guru Rinpoche mantras. My wife also offered 100,000 prostrations and recited the mantras. For a while she postponed the mandala offerings, but eventually she was able to accomplish this practice as well. Then we journeyed together to a cave called Kya-Shuk, the former retreat of Repa Shiwa Ö, a famed disciple of Milarepa. There we stayed and practiced for the entire winter season. During the winter my wife became pregnant, and when spring came she returned to her family and I returned to my lama.

The monastery of my teacher, Naptra Rinpoche, was situated on a slope of a mountain range consisting of seven peaks, which the locals called "The Seven Brothers." The mountain on which my lama's monastery was located was named Butra Pundun. Two shimmering lakes adorned this mountain: White Lake and Black Lake. A local folksong refers to these lakes: "In the holy mountain range of Tsipri, do not say there are no gems; if the White Lake and the Black Lake are not precious gems, what then can be called a jewel?"

During my stay there, I met and learned from many special lamas. Sukhang Lama of Langkor taught me the Chöd melody and the accompanying dance. Later, when we were practicing alone, he gave me many more transmissions from the Chöd tradition, including the Chöd tsok Rinchen Trengwa. He also gave me the rare tradition, to which I still adhere, coming directly from Padampa Sangye.

Kham Dzogchen lama, who was called Sangye Norbu, gave me the transmission for Tsok and for the perfection of wisdom sutras and the practice for the Tsering Che Nga Long life sisters.

There was great practitioner called Dawa from Tsipri. One day, Dawa took me to look after his sheep. When we found a private place, he gave me the Cherezig Jowo Tukje Chenpo empowerments and instructions on how to meditate. After this teaching, I practiced diligently until suddenly Chenrezig appeared in the sky in front of me, just like watching a movie. I can still see this very clearly, even today.

Aku Trasang and Aku Norbu were both great teachers in Naptra's monastery. They gave me the transmission for Longchen Nyingthig.

Chamang Kushu Pema provided me with the transmission for Chenrezig and Guru Rinpche's mantra.

Kuye Chonyi was another important lama for me.

Aku Jigme of Tingri taught me the ritual to offer smoke and incense, and Aku Tsultrim taught me Shenyi Druptob, which is a puja for helping people overcome illness.

Kum Trul gave me Guru Rinpoche's transmission and empowerment.

Tedun Tsering Wangdu gave me long life empowerments.

Lama Mukre gave me the transmission for Guru Trakpo, a wrathful form of Guru Rinpoche.

Bumtang Sonam gave me the empowerment and transmission for Riwo Sangcho, a smoke offering, and the Changter transmission.

Traktul Rinpoche gave me the transmission and empowerment for Mahakala.

Kari Rinpoche gave me the transmission for Mimetsepa and Vajrayogini from the Gelugpa tradition.

Chupsang Rinpoche from Tsipri gave me Ngultrul Dharmabadra's teachings and practice called Trakpo Sum Dil.

Sochen Omze gave me the empowerment for Namtrak Choku.

Ponlop Champa gave me the empowerment for the 21 Taras.

Some other lamas who were important to me were Chapuk Tulku, Choten Nyimei' Lama, Tedun Tsering Wangdu, Tsaribuk lama, Gomchen Lungdok, Lama Kagyud, Gomchen Ugyen, Gomchen Kampa, Gomchen Goyukpa, and Trülshik Rinpoche.

One day when we sat together, my lama spoke to me intently. "Normally, students have to do three sets of preliminary practices before receiving certain teachings, but this year is very important. Even though you've completed only two sets, I'm going to give you an initiation immediately. There is no time to waste."

After receiving special teachings called explanations, tsa-lung (channel practices), and Powa (transference of consciousness), lama gave me the full empowerment, transmissions, and explanations for Chöd practice. Then he sent me and some forty other disciples to the mountains for a seven-day retreat, with only our ritual instruments – the kangling, or thighbone trumpet, and damaru, a hand-held drum.

While we were staying by the White Lake and Black Lake, huge hailstorms appeared suddenly as a sign of our practice. After a week had passed, all the other students were sent back to their homes, but lama said I should remain there alone and practice for an extra three days. Afterward, he asked me to come to his place, where he offered me a large ritual cake. "Now we have studied Chöd practice for one month and then practiced it in the mountains for ten days," he said. "In western Tibet, where I come from, it is our tradition to visit one hundred eight funeral grounds for Chöd practice, over a period of three months and ten days." With these words my lama sent me off on a remarkable journey.

The Journey Begins

Ascending from the monastery toward the holy mountain range of Tsipri, it is necessary to cross a pass named Chang La. Along the ridge there was a sacred funeral ground near a monastery known as Singatrak. Here I stayed the night in the home of one Aku Sangpo.

Aku Sangpo lived with his mother, prepared tea for visitors, and cared for the temple. Another of his jobs was to continually turn the prayer wheel while his friends read religious texts. He was a very generous man and also very talkative.

"You must be tired carrying your backpack," he said. "Let us have a good pot of tea and you can stay the night." While Sangpo and I talked about Buddhism, his mother opened up a small pot of butter and took out half of it to make tea for us, leaving the other half in the courtyard. She brought us our refreshments, and stayed to listen to our discussion. Soon we heard a great tumult coming from the courtyard, but we remained absorbed in our conversation.

When the mother left us and returned to the courtyard to make more tea, she discovered that all the butter had vanished, carried away by birds. Returning to us with the empty pot in her hand, she exclaimed, "There is no butter left! It has all been eaten by ravens!" Her son scolded her for not taking care of the provisions, but I thought this was an ironic omen.

"We just talked of Chöd practice," I told Sangpo, "where the entire body, the blood and the flesh, are all given up as alms. What could it matter if one pot, half full of butter, was lost?"

"That's right!" he said – and we all broke into laughter.

After eating dinner I went to the funeral ground to practice. I stayed one night without receiving any special signs. But, very early the next morning, some distance from me, I saw a small spark of light, like a small fire. Investigating, I found a little, bright white stone in the shape of a conch. I took this as a sign of auspiciousness and have kept this object to this day.

Next I went to Dzomo Korwa in Tsipri Mountain. The village there was called Ne-Sar, and I visited the local monastery, called Chuzang. Here I was able to pay homage to a Tara statue called "Sang-Sum Drolma-Sum Chu," the Three Secret Places of the Thirty Taras. This statue was reputed to have actually spoken. I also visited the holy funeral sites in Charok Dzong.

From there I traveled on to Shelkar monastery, which was on the west side of the mountain. I circumambulated the entire mountain and visited a cemetery site called Dupde. Crossing the mountain pass, I came across another burial ground named Lolo. A hot spring bubbled from the ground in this place, and above it was a large and handsome cave. There, living as a hermit, was a man called Geshe. The local people had strong faith in this simple man, who was very tall and dressed in a lay person's garb. His only companions were three sheep who lived in front of the cave and survived on grass and leftover tea leaves. Indeed, there were always three large tea pots simmering in the Geshe's cave, even though he lived alone. He always served delicious tea, insisting that his visitors drank generous servings. If anyone offered him money or alms, he would just give these to the monastery to buy butter lamps. The only holy object he owned was a stone statue of Tara. He took care of this so meticulously that it was completely coated with the oil he used to clean it.

"This is my most sacred object," he informed me. I asked him to give me some teachings, to which he replied, "I don't know much about Chöd, but I can offer you a Tara practice, since this is my main deity." Geshe then advised me, "If you are going to funeral grounds to

44

practice Chöd, you will need blankets and clothes, as well as animals to carry your things." Later, after taking a hot spring bath, I asked for alms from the people in that area who offered me barley flour for my ongoing journey.

Terrifying Places

In Shelkar, there was a river tributary where people threw the bodies of the dead. Wealthier individuals brought their dead to holier sites such as Dupde, but here, the people were poor and just threw the corpses into the open river. I stayed there a single night and had some frightening experiences. It is possibly the most terrifying funeral site I have ever visited. First of all, during the night there were many strange whistling sounds emanating from the place. Later, four or five wolves appeared out of the darkness, and then several corpses seemed to fall down the slope almost on top of me. When I went to look the next morning, I found only three large stones, not dead bodies!

Following the route from Zambuling Pass toward Gotsang, I arrived at a rock cave in the middle of Tsipri Mountain. The wind was so powerful, and there was so much dust in the air, that I had to take refuge for a while behind a large rock. The next day I became ill and had to force myself to keep walking. I continued to a small mountain called Kunzöm Gyalpo. Though prayer flags fluttered from the peak, it was still a very frightening spot. As I tried to climb higher, two skeletons came rushing down toward me. I thought, "Is this a dream or is this real?" and I immediately took out my kangling and damaru and began to practice. Just then a blinding dust storm rose up, and the demons were lost from view.

On the mountaintop I set up my tent to practice the Chöd ritual, but a strong gale rose up and sent my tent sailing down the slope. I knew I would not be able to follow it at the rate it was moving, so I decided to just let it go. I remained on the mountain, continuing to practice.

Then in the early morning hours I dreamed that a man dressed in white appeared and put a gift on my pillow. When I awoke, I found a white bag with some barley and five or six Tibetan coins. Since it seemed to have fallen from the prayer flags, I returned it to its former place. Later I went to search for my tent and found it deep in the woods, half buried by sand. Fortunately, I was able to salvage it and started off again.

One day, I came across a nun walking with ten or fifteen sheep and reciting prayers. "Each of my sheep has a name," she said to me, looking at them fondly. I immediately remembered the Geshe's advice about the need for an animal to carry my blankets and food.

"I am going to visit one hundred eight funeral sites for my Chöd practice," I said. "I need some sheep to help carry my things. Can you offer me one or two?"

"I love my sheep too much," she said. "I cannot possibly give any away."

We walked together toward the local monastery, called Kyetsang Gompa, chatting along the way. "I am a Khampa and I do like Chöd," she said. "If you are a practitioner, will you do a ritual for me?" So I performed Chöd and the ritual Chöd dance or cham. She was delighted and gave me a small bag of barley flour. Looking at me directly, she said, "Now I know you are an honest practitioner and you won't eat my sheep if I give one to you. My oldest sheep is called Tharchin

Norbu (Jewel who has Reached the End Goal). He eats only barley flour; you must look after him well." Saying this, she showed me her oldest sheep. He was very large with huge horns, a white body, and a black face and feet.

This clever sheep could actually understand my words. If I said, "Go and eat grass," it would do just that, and if I said, "Come here and go to sleep," it would follow my command.

I discovered that at the monastery there was a high lama named Tripön Rinpoche. That night I took my new sheep, Norbu, to stay with a monk who lived in a cave just below Kyetsang Monastery. The next day I went to visit the Rinpoche, but unfortunately, he was on retreat. He sent me a message through his attendants, saying that I should see another lama nearby. He explained, "It is the same thing as seeing me." And so I prepared to meet Kushap Lama. When I visited him, he was eating cakes with a bag of barley flour next to him. He was not very old, and appeared to be a native of Kham.

"Where are you from?" he inquired.

"I am a disciple of Naptra Rinpoche, who has instructed me to visit one hundred eight funeral sites. Can you give me any transmissions or practices?"

"This is wonderful," he said. "This is the first time I have heard of a practitioner from Tingri doing this practice of one hundred eight sites. If you can fulfill your master's wishes, that is enough. I don't have any other instructions to give you." He then handed me a long protection cord. "If you are going to accomplish this practice, there will be many difficulties. Please also take this barley flour." I noticed that he didn't look very rich, living more like a simple yogi.

"I have enough, thank you," I told him, and returned his gift of flour.

"You seem to be very special," he said. "It is auspicious to have met you." And those were his parting words.

Sheep Adventures

I was supposed to complete my visits to the funeral sites within three months and ten days, but on my return journey I still had ten days left. Arriving at a place called Tsakor, I practiced on a huge rock just below the village. While I was doing my practice, a Nepali woman dressed in red appeared. She said, "I will bring grass for your sheep."

"Perfect. My sheep needs food," I replied. She also gave me a handful of snow pea flowers. I was really surprised to see these greens, as it was still winter and everything was a parched yellow and brown. I tied the flowers onto the central pole of my tent, and the next morning, thinking this must have been a vision, I arose to see whether they were actually there. They were still tied to the pole. I gave the grass to my sheep Tharchin Norbu, and kept one piece for myself as a holy object, to remind me of my meeting with this magical being. Much later, when I visited Nepal, I recognized these snow pea flowers. She must have traveled a very long way.

From Tsakor I traveled five hours to Pangri. A family there invited me to stay and gave me noodle soup and tea. Crossing the pass behind Pangri village, I reached the Patrug Valley. There I found a funeral site called Gyasha. Although the people simply called it by this name, the local monks told me its meaning was actually "the hat of one hundred holy sites." This was a very pleasant spot, and it was said that a disciple of Milarepa, Shiwa Ö, had stayed there. In this isolated place, water had to be brought up from below. I stayed there for four days. There were two old meditators here, as well as four or five nuns. Everybody was drinking millet wine and I drank along with them.

One of the yogis remarked upon the agility of my sheep. "Your animal is very great; he can climb up and down mountains and follow you to many holy places. He is very lucky to be staying with you. What is his name?"

"Tharchin Norbu," I said.

The meditator continued speaking. "He is just an animal – whether he will reach enlightenment or not I don't know. But because it is very auspicious that he is traveling with you, a Chöd practitioner, I will rename him Kalsang Norbu." This means Jewel of Good Fortune.

But when I addressed my sheep as Kalsang Norbu it did not respond, so I just kept calling him Tharchin Norbu. This sheep knew its own mind!

From there I went down to Tragdu, where there were two lamas. One gave me blessed pills and said, "You are accomplishing your lama's wishes, and this is very meaningful. We cannot offer you anything more than this." I gave one blessing pill to my sheep.

After that I went to a place called Drongkha. Khari Gompa, a Gelugpa monastery and nunnery, was situated here. The lama, Khari Rinpoche, had been a monk at Shelkar, but had left there in order to live here in the small village. The people regarded him highly. This lama invited me to stay at his monastery and asked his nuns to make tea for me. He was very talkative but did not seem fond of animals.

"This isn't so good, you must keep your sheep outside," he said. But when I left Norbu outside, he started to bleat continually, "Baaaahhhh, baaahhh." This woke the Rinpoche, who said, "Your sheep is a big problem. It is not sleeping, it is just crying." I told him that it must be allowed inside, because without me it would be lonely and cry. So I took the sheep into Rinpoche's room. But being a sheep, it defecated in his room all night!

In spite of this difficult beginning, the Rinpoche generously offered me wonderful food and tea during my stay. As it turned out, Khari Rinpoche had received the quintessential Dzogchen instructions from Rongphu Sangye together with my lama, Naptra Rinpoche, at Dza Rongphu.

He asked, "How many disciples does Naptra Rinpoche have receiving teachings?"

"About five hundred in Saga Dawa," I replied.

He became very happy upon hearing this, rejoicing in the success of Naptra Rinpoche. He then said, "Naptra Rinpoche is a very compassionate, good lama, and maybe he is flourishing with many students because of the blessings Rongphu Sangye gave him the key to the Longchen Nyingthig. There has never been such a gathering of these teachings here before."

"There are no funeral sites here," he added, "but farther up the mountain there is a place where we offer prayer flags to two protector deities. This can be a terrifying place at night. You can certainly do your Chöd up there." The two protector deities Khari Rinpoche referred to are Tashi Öbar, the protector deity of Shelkar Gompa and Tashi Lhunpo, and a very wrathful local deity named Phagpa Khari, the Noble of Sky Mountain. Following his suggestion, I went up the mountain with Norbu and did my practice, but alas, no manifestations arose. After I came down the next morning, Khari Rinpoche offered me some Tibetan coins and sent me on my way.

From there I passed by a nomadic village and crossed over a high pass that overlooked my native region. Near the pass, I met a man who told me he was of the Shekyi Nelung clan, a well-to-do family from Tingri village. We walked together, but before reaching the man's village we arrived at a holy place called Tsari Buk. He told me, "If you're going to stay here tonight at Tsari Buk cave, you're welcome to my home tomorrow." I agreed, but because I had some very heavy blankets with me, I asked him to take them to his village on his horse, where I could pick them up later.

The caretaker of this holy place was a lay practitioner who had an old woman as his wife. He invited me to stay for one day, and they prepared a great feast. Later he told me that he was the son of the lama called Kushu Gyaltsen, whom I had invited to make tsok offerings when I was the Shika official. When I explained to him who I was, he became quite excited and happily showed me a secret room under the cave where there were many ancient statues and stupas. The next day he accompanied me to the village.

I then went to retrieve my blankets from the man I had met earlier. But his family in Tsari Buk village told me that he had gone to the mountains and was not home. They refused to return my possessions, even after the caretaker requested this on my behalf. It turned out that the man I had met was not so well off after all, though he had a rich family's last name! Even if he were at home, he probably wouldn't have returned them. Thus I lost all my blankets.

The Sky Burial

I did my Chöd practices near Tingri village in a place called Nechung Pula in Singatrak, and from there I went to a cave of Machik Labdron that I had visited previously. I rested there for two or three days. From this cave I then crossed the pass of Tingri-Khangmar to a place called Duntsa. Soon I arrived at the Langkor funeral site. It was said to be a frightening place, but I did not find it to be fearsome at all – there was only the sound of wild jackals. The next day someone brought the corpse of an old man for a sky burial, in which vultures are called to consume the dead body as it is chopped into pieces. I reflected on the impermanence of life and performed a cham dance and Chöd ritual.

Because I had never seen how a corpse was handled, I stayed to watch. First they removed the clothes and placed the body on a stone, with its head facing down. I asked the funeral monk, "Why don't you put the corpse facing the west, as is traditionally done? Why do you place it facing down?"

"We are facing the corpse towards Padampa Sangye's monastery in Langkor below us," he explained.

While the corpse lay there, the workers drank rice beer and feasted. Then they removed their ordinary clothes and put on cloaks and took out their knives. First they cut off the back of the corpse. They took out all the muscles and flesh and left the bones and the other remains there. They packed this into a heavy blanket and put it aside.

By now all the vultures in the area were waiting in a circle around the body. Addressing these birds, the funeral monk commanded, "Now take this offering." The ravens had also come, but they were not allowed to eat. The vultures stuck out their necks, but did not eat the body yet. When I asked why, the monk explained, "The king bird who is the owner of this place has not yet come." Nearby they offered barley flour and incense, facing the west.

Just then the king bird flew down from a rocky ridge and approached the site, flying in a peculiar manner. When the king bird landed, its wings made a unique "shhhhhhhh" sound. The funeral monk reported who it was who had died, and the bird responded by cawing, "Arwkkk Arwkkk."

The monk explained, "When the bird lands and makes the sound 'shhhhh,' the bird means to say, 'Who is that person?' and I report the name of the dead individual. When the bird makes the sound 'Arwkk Arwkk' it means 'I'm sorry for your loss.'"

Then the king bird started to peck at the body, and all the other birds joined in and began to feed. Most of the bones were devoured easily with snaps of their powerful beaks. Except for the head and the bones of the feet, they ate everything in less then ten minutes.

The monk smashed several of the remaining bones into pieces and mixed this with the flesh they had put aside earlier. This was eaten within a single minute by the ravenous birds. At last, only a few bones remained. They put these remaining bones into a very oily-looking concave-shaped rock and pounded them with a stone. The head was then put into the rock and beaten and mashed. Mixing the bones with the brains, they also fed this to the vultures. They completely swarmed over this mixture, as if it were some kind of delicacy.

Except for four or five pieces of skeleton that the birds were unable to eat, the whole body was now gone. In the woods just near the funeral site, they burned these remaining bones in a fire. The birds were satiated, and just stood around the site, preening their feathers. The funeral workers gave the dead man's belongings, such as his clothes and other small objects, to the water carriers.

Subduing Dogs

After that I went to a village called Shingri with two other monks. There I again practiced my Chöd ritual, the "Laughter of the Dakinis." The next day we walked to a great and vast nomadic place. Nomads typically own large dogs, and as we approached, three big mastiffs came charging at us. I had my sheep with me, but it seemed that they were not interested in him at all, only in biting us! I took my tent pole and tried to block them, but they charged in. They were huge! I visualized the wrathful deity, Troma Nagmo, and I charged right back at the dogs. I hit one on the head with my tent pole shouting, "Hah!" and I hit it so hard, it was knocked unconscious. but then the dog woke up, staggering as if drunk. The other dogs immediately retreated.

After that, all the nomads came running down to meet us. Instead of being angry as I expected, they said, "It was very fortunate you were able to hit that dog. No one can ever get near it. It always chases people, and has hurt many, even if they are riding a horse. Even just now it was tied with an iron chain, but just look at how it broke free."

The nomads were kind and generous. They took the dogs away and gave us a half body of mutton.

At the time, although we had not witnessed it ourselves, we had heard news of Chinese forces and Tibetans fighting in the west. There was much talk with the nomads about this. The other monk I was traveling with remarked, "You are so strong. If you can subdue this dog, you can subdue ten Chinese fighters."

They asked me to come with them to Kyirong in the west, but as I was looking forward to the reunion with my lama, I did not join them on their march to battle. The monk and I divided the meat in half and parted ways.

The Great Flood

On my way back, I passed a river that flowed into a small lake, with large mountains looming above it. Just near the riverbank, I collected some dry wood from the forest, set up a fire and began to boil the mutton. When the meat was almost cooked, I looked up and saw a mass of black clouds forming in the sky. Glancing down, I saw what appeared to be a white horse racing toward me. Thinking this was just an apparition created by local deities, I got out my damaru and kangling and began to practice under the darkening skies. But when I looked again, I realized it was not a horse at all, but a massive wall of water. A flash flood on the river!

I chased my sheep to safety as the river swelled and overflowed the banks. My pot and meat were all washed away – only my tent was left. My damaru and practice objects were drenched, and my other possessions had disappeared downstream. Scrambling for higher ground, I saw a small white house and a cave. Hoping somebody might live there, I made my way up the hill with my walking stick and my sheep.

Just before reaching the cave and house, I arrived at a pasture surrounded by a stone wall. I spread my tent on the wall to dry, but was unable to lie down to rest there because of all the sheep dung in the field, so I sat in the meditation posture of Buddha Vairochana.

At dusk I saw someone approaching me, a man wearing a white chuba with braided hair and bangs in front. One sleeve was taken off, and he was carrying water in a clay pot, suspended in a rope net. I thought he must be one of the residents of the house perched high above. But when he came close to where I had left my tent, he seemed to vanish. I got up to look for him but found nothing. Later I heard a sound like stones falling where I had put my tent to dry. I assumed it was water dripping from the wet material.

When I awoke the next morning, I had no further visions, but as I was packing up my shelter, I noticed a dead body lying in the midst of the stones – an abandoned corpse. Was this the form I had seen coming down the hill? I went to the lakeside and did Chöd and the cham dance.

Later I met two very tall women who were milking their yaks. The eldest of them complained of a toothache and requested that I perform a mantra for her affliction. Afterward she was pleased and offered me tea.

"You were lucky you did not die in the flood. We call this the man-eating river," she said. "Many people have died because of it." This name apparently was because of the wrathful activity of the deity of Pongrong monastery, a place I had visited earlier.

From here, there was nowhere else for me to go. In the west, the road met Kyirang Pass, so there was nothing for me to do but turn back.

I stayed at Shapkar for the night. There I met a highly religious couple, who lived with their only daughter. Their house was very humble, just a small sheep barn with a simple roof. The father's work was inscribing mantras on stone. Because of their strong Buddhist faith, they requested that I stay and practice Chöd. They told me, "If you go up this hill you will find Peptse cave, which was Milarepa's hermitage. If you stay there, we will serve you food for a month." But their devotion went even further. "We have only one daughter," they said, and they asked me to marry this very virtuous girl.

But because my pilgrimage was about to end, I had to postpone any such decision. "First I must go to see my lama and I will do whatever he instructs me," I said. "Later I will come back to practice in this cave."

Water Demons

On the return journey, I went to Nacholing monastery, near the headwaters of a great river. The lama there invited me to his room, explaining that his statue made noises at night; he requested that I perform a Chöd ritual for him. He was a Nyingmapa, who had also received transmissions and empowerments from my own lama. He kindly told me, "You have been to many different places. You must be tired. You can rest here."

I stayed to do the ritual and he offered me a large ritual feast with yogurt and other food cooked by his sister, who was a nun. The monastery was situated near the source of this river called Bumchu, meaning "the water that comes from a vase." Though this was the correct name, some call it Bong-Chu, which means "donkey water." Above the river, there was a stupa called Bumpa which means "the vase." Below the stupa, water pours out directly from the rocks of the mountainside, and people regard this spring as very sacred. The lama said, "This is the source of the Bumchu River, which flows into India. You should do Chöd practice here for one night. You may have a scary encounter."

I performed a Chöd practice and cham dance as he had suggested. In the beginning no manifestations occurred, but after some time a naga, a snake-like creature who dwells underground or in water, appeared. With jet-black skin, his lower body was that of a snake and remained still, while the upper body writhed fiercely. His face was wrathful with large dog-like teeth, through which he was shouting loudly. I addressed the naga demon, saying, "Don't worry, if you are hungry I will give you my flesh, if you are thirsty I will give you my blood."

The naga spoke. "I won't take your body, but I will take your blood." In my meditation I offered him blood from my fingers.

In typical Chöd visualizations, one gives both blood and flesh to the demons. One visualizes turning one's own blood into milk and offers it to harmful spirits and other beings. It's a way of extending compassion to the demons and spirits that can afflict man. After the naga's thirst was quenched, he entered back into the river. When only his head was still above the water, he said to me, "This blood is not enough, I will drink more."

As he disappeared below the surface, two young men with horses suddenly appeared in the place where the naga had been. Their hair was braided up in traditional style, and they were engaged in a fight with knives. One was badly wounded, and a great deal of blood spilled from his body.

The next morning I went back to the lama who had suggested I practice there and reported my experience. Then I packed my bags and left the monastery.

Years later, when people from that area came to Kathmandu, I inquired of them about this place, and they related what had happened there. Twenty years after my visit there, the Chinese relaxed their anti-religious policies, and people were allowed to put up prayer flags again. But a fight broke out over a land dispute, and a man was killed on that very spot. My vision had been a prophecy of this murder.

Birds and Another Dog

In this area, there were many nomads who lived in tents. As I was traveling east, I encountered some old nomadic ruins. I had heard these places were frightening, so I went there to do my Chöd practice. An old man appeared to me, wearing a sheepskin coat and a yellow hat, spinning a prayer wheel. He asked me, "What are you doing here?" I thought he must be the deity of the place. I said, "I am practicing Chöd."

"Well," he replied, "If you want to practice Chöd, you must practice in the rocky places over there." Then he walked away.

In the early morning when I was getting up, eight or nine crane-like Khongmo birds arrived and landed where I was. These beautiful birds surrounded me, and we just sat together in this uninhabited place for a while.

When the sun rose higher in the sky, I began my journey once more. But as I was leaving this rocky area, another mad dog charged at me. This was definitely real, and not a vision! Protecting myself with my walking stick, I tried to lose him, but he kept chasing me. It took two or three hours before I was able to get rid of him by hiding behind a sand hill, while the dog sniffed along the riverside. From my hiding place I could see the dog run off toward some nomads who were tending their yaks.

I next went to a place with some ruined old houses and many prayer flags. That night I stayed in an old barn and did my Chöd ritual and cham dances. Nothing extraordinary happened that night, except for the sound of a conch shell blowing two or three times. In the morning, I woke at sunrise and went to see the prayer flags and ruins. Right at the base of the stupa where people put the prayer flags, I found a very beautiful statue of Ganesh. It must have been there since ancient times. I remember this image profoundly, and even now Ganesh is a deity with special significance to me.

The Fruits of Virtue and Non-Virtue

I stayed with an old yogi at Trakar monastery who asked me to do Chöd in his home. He was very happy with my practice and said, "I have a lot of tea, please stay here. Tomorrow I will take you to see the sacred objects in the monastery." Because it was a very old monastery, there were many ancient statues and paintings. "In Trakar there is a funeral ground with a flat stone that is said to have come all the way from India. This is a frightful place, a place where you should practice Chöd."

He escorted me to the site, and indeed the flat rock situated on the slope of the hill was the size of a large room. And it had a crack straight down the middle. I asked him about the split in the rock. "At one time a simple butcher was buried here, but because of his impurities, the rock broke in half. Also a lama's body was cremated on that very stone," he said.

"Was it the simple person's funeral or the heat of the lama's fire that broke the rock?" I asked. This he did not know.

I told him, "In the Dharma there is no low or high – all are equal. There is only a good heart and a bad heart. The rock was not broken because of the butcher; it seems that there were just too many fires. In the future, please do not talk about low-caste people in this way. Educated people will not believe you. You should say the rock broke from too many fires." To this the yogi agreed.

Because I was unable to pitch my tent on that massive stone, I simply laid the tent down and used it as a seat, and this is where I performed Chöd. The rock carried a foul smell from all the sky burials, the grisly residue of broken bones and human fat. That night while I was practicing, jackals, foxes, and wild cats appeared from all directions, making rough and frightening noises. I visualized offering my flesh and blood and then fell deeply asleep. In my dreams, a man appeared wearing an all-white coat.

We started to argue, and this soon broke into a fight. I grabbed him by the hair and held him tightly. Waking with a start, I saw that it was already dawn. When I looked down at my hand, it was full of human hair! I had thought this was a dream, but the hair was very real! As I packed my things that morning I looked all around the stone. I discovered that when they performed the funeral rites they cut the hair off and placed it below the rock, feeding the rest of the corpse to the vultures. I returned to the old yogi and recounted what had happened.

"That's right," he said, "just a few days ago a shepherd died. Maybe his mind is still attached to that place." I instructed them that in the future, the funeral ceremony should include burning the hair as well. Nothing should be left behind.

But he told me their reasoning. "We believe that because the stone flew here from India thousands of years ago, if we put the hair under the rock then the mind will be blessed."

"It doesn't work like that," I explained. "It is the fruits of virtuous or non-virtuous actions that benefit the mind, not an earthly stone or the hair of a deceased person. When you clean the body's flesh and bones, you must also get rid of the hair."

The yogi understood my words and meaning. However, I do not know whether they followed my admonitions, as I have never been able return to this place.

Giving Birth

The next day, as I traveled along the road, a young woman suddenly came running toward me. "Why are you in such a hurry?" I asked.

"I have a friend who is pregnant and has stomach pain. I'm afraid she might die. There is no one else available, and I hoped you would be able to help." I followed her and found her friend in a barn nearby, sweating profusely. Feeling great compassion in my heart, I practiced a healing Chöd ritual for her.

As soon as I had finished and put my damaru away, the baby was born. "I need to cut the cord," the woman said hurriedly. I held the blankets while she searched for a suitable knife. The baby's little body was shivering, and the mother just lay there completely spent, as if she were dead. A string was tied to the cord in two places and the knife was used to cut it in the center, causing a little blood to spurt out.

"Is the baby all right or was she hurt?" I asked.

"The baby is fine," she said. She wrapped the infant in white blankets and brought it to the resting mother. The woman fed the exhausted mother with some barley flour and butter porridge, and she was then able to breast feed the child. She requested that I stay the night, but I said I had to go. The kind woman offered me some wool and what little butter she had.

I told her, "I do not know how to spin or do anything with the wool, so I have no use for it. Furthermore, the mother needs this butter much more than I do." Thus I refused her offerings and went on my way.

Realization

After a while I reached a place with a stone wall. That night it rained so heavily that my tent and blankets were completely soaked through. It was so cold that my teeth chattered and I felt completely down-trodden and hopeless. After a very long night, dawn finally came and the sun rose. I attempted to squeeze the water from my drenched blanket and tent, and spread them on the stone wall with my clothing to dry. I pulled myself up onto a big rock and sat completely naked, trying to warm up in the sun.

While meditating in this way, I suddenly realized the nature of impermanence. Yesterday I had blankets and a damaru and now I couldn't use either of them. Now, I was just as naked as the day I was born. I began to think of how Milarepa or Dampa Sangye never possessed a damaru or any such things, so why did I need them?

I felt so happy and free that I started singing out loud. Before long, I was singing and dancing around on top of that rock, stark naked. Just then, three men and two women came toward me. The first man said to the others in a frightened voice, "Oh no! Look, there is a dead body, but it is moving about!"

"I'm not a corpse!" I called to them. "I'm a man!"

"It's a demon, it's a demon!" They screamed and scattered down the hill. I laughed so hard I nearly fell off my boulder!

My possessions eventually dried out, but my supply of barley flour had been spoiled. Looking up, I spotted a column of smoke coming from a distant hill. As I was heading toward this source of human habitation – and food – I met an unkempt old woman. She didn't invite me into her tent, but instead brought out a yak skin and asked me to sit outside. She offered me a cup of tea and some yogurt with barley flour, and then asked me to recite the prayers of Tara. I agreed.

Afterward, I said to her, "I am a Chöd practitioner, so if you like, I can perform this ritual for you as well."

"Oh I don't need a Chöd ritual," she said confidently. "The Tara puja is enough for me." In return for the recitation of the Tara puja, she offered me a leg of mutton.

"The meat is good," I said, "but it would be more practical if you gave me barley flour for my journey, because I don't have any left." And so I took leave of the woman and her tent, replenished with a large bag of flour.

From here I went to a lake on top of a hill. It was a very pleasant and peaceful place to practice. The sun was warm, the grass was soft, and it didn't rain, and I felt so at ease that I lay down and napped naked in the sunshine. That night I could hear the lake water lapping gently at the shore. I did my Chöd practice without any manifestations appearing.

The next morning as I was leaving, a rabbit appeared on the road and seemed to block my way. If I moved to the right, it would also move this way. If I moved to the left, it would move in front of me again. Though at first I wondered if this was some kind of manifestation, I finally discerned that this rabbit was actually blind and just responding to the sounds of my movement!

Lama's Predictions

I arrived back at my lama's monastery around noon; it was exactly three months and ten days since I had left. When I reached the bottom of the hill, I sent a message informing Rinpoche that I had returned. Rinpoche sent a message back saying that I shouldn't meet him that night. The message read: "It is not auspicious to come in the evening. Tomorrow morning is better – come up when you hear the thighbone trumpet."

But many of my dharma friends had already heard of my arrival, and they came down to greet me. Some brought noodles; others brought dried tea, foods, and many other kinds of gifts.

"Why are you staying down here?" they asked. "Come to our room." These people were not aware that I had been visiting funeral grounds for many months, because Rinpoche had sent me on this pilgrimage secretly. "You have lost weight and your skin is so dark. What happened to you?"

I told them I had been sick. "If you are sick, come sleep in our home, we have a nice place for you."

"I don't feel like sleeping in a room. I have become a little crazy," I said, "I will just stay in my tent." When they heard this they thought it was very strange, and they soon left.

When the sun rose the next morning I packed everything up and just waited. It was several hours – after ten o'clock – before Rinpoche signaled and I heard the sound of the kangling.

As I walked slowly toward the sound, I felt an odd mixture of happiness and depression. Leaving my bags at the door of the monastery, I went straight to see my lama, which is the tradition. However, he immediately asked, "Where is your bag?"

"At the door," I said.

"Bring it here," he instructed. Rinpoche was sitting on a throne and had arranged a seat for me as well. His attendants brought me tea and he offered me a plate of rock sugar, from which I took one or two pieces. He then told an attendant to open up my bag.

Rinpoche examined the contents, looking over my tent and blankets. Then he began to recite many prayers. His face became very red and he gazed up at the open sky as he performed inner visualizations, his hands shifting into many sacred shapes or mudras.

Rinpoche noted the good quantity of barley flour and meat in my bag. He asked, "What is all that?"

"I met an old woman on the way who gave me a lot of food. I have been eating only this for two days and this is what is left over."

"Well, you didn't have any problems with food, did you?" Rinpoche laughed.

He asked me many questions about my practice, what I had done, what experiences I had had, and all the different places I had been. I reported everything.

Meaningful Events

"What was the most challenging experience for your mind?" he asked me.

"At the tributary just below Shelkar village, corpses were falling like rocks into the river and I nearly fell in myself. At that place, I had the most difficult experience."

"It's a meeting place of three rivers," Rinpoche explained, "and it's a holy place of Dorje Phagmo. So you were blessed by Dorje Phagmo there."

I told him about encountering the two skeletons, and how I became terrified, my body rigid with fear. Rinpoche reflected on this carefully for a moment.

"If these two skeletons were coming up to receive you, and if you were going down, it would be auspicious. But in your case you were ascending, while the skeletons were descending. This is not a good sign; it means you will not have many disciples." In my case they were not only descending, he said, but had also vanished. If I had performed dances with these skeletons, it would have created causes for a much better outcome.

I then reported to Rinpoche about the different lamas I had met.

"This is very good," he said. "You have done very well."

I told him of the time I attempted to meet a high lama who happened to be on retreat, and I instead met his friend, who was eating a simple but hearty meal.

"The higher lamas will always be good to you," said Rinpoche.

I related to him how I had asked someone to carry my blankets, and the man's family then refused to give them back.

"That's no problem," he said. "When you practice Dharma, obstacles will arise. This obstacle has been carried away with him. For a long time, you must practice compassion for this person and not indulge in anger or jealousy."

Next, I described the funeral activities at Langkor and how they fed the body to the birds.

"That's good. Langkor is your birthplace; it is a good sign that you saw all these funeral activities. But if you had seen a woman's corpse it would have been more auspicious."

I recounted the story of Pongrong village and the large dog that attacked me.

"Your root practice is Dorje Phagmo, Vajrayogini in wrathful form. You should practice that."

I told him of the flood that washed everything away.

"That is a sign that you will live in another country one day."

I explained about the corpse I found in the field, amongst the rocks and sheep dung.

"That is a sign that in the future you will not have problems getting food, clothing, and wealth."

I told Rinpoche about the rock engravers who asked me to stay and marry their daughter.

"It is a sign that you will be separated from the wife you have now."

I related about the lama who gave me a feast.

"In the future you will meet many lamas who will help you practice Dharma."

I also mentioned meeting the Khongmo birds and the rabbit that blocked my way.

"This indicates that you will help many poor and sick people."

I told him about seeing the white statue of Ganesh.

"The gods of wealth will favor you. If you visit people's houses you will bring good fortune to them."

I continued and told him about meeting the pregnant woman.

"You will later come across many more situations like this."

I then reported about the old woman who gave me barley flour and meat.

"This is a sign that the deities will always take care of you."

I recounted my experience at the flat rock, and the hair in my hand after I woke up from fighting with a man in a white coat.

"It's a sign that many people will be jealous of you, but your practice will be as real as gold."

Next I told him about the woman who gave me the flowers in winter.

"This is a sign that at the end of your life you will be in a place that has harvests in both summer and winter."

Finally, I told him about the nun who gave me the sheep.

"This indicates that you will always be happy and have mental equipoise."

Rinpoche then told me that he had met a certain caretaker – the son of the Rinpoche I had previously invited to give empowerments in Shika. The caretaker had recounted the tale of the man who stole my blankets, adding a concluding chapter. That summer, a severe lightning storm had swept over the region. During that time, the man was struck by lightning and killed on the spot. Not only did he die, but many of his sheep had been killed as well. "Did you do this with black magic?" Rinpoche asked.

"No, I did not. This is against my practice. Actually I felt great compassion for him."

In this way Rinpoche explained each and every event I had experienced. He then questioned me, "Has fearlessness arisen in your mind?"

"Yes. There is no fear in my mind or heart; I do not have materialistic grasping. I don't feel partiality toward good or bad, clean or dirty."

Again he asked, "Do you have equanimity of mind, free from excitement and lethargy?"

"Yes, I have exactly that feeling," I replied.

"This state of mind is very difficult to accomplish. From this state, the enlightened mind is easy to find. If you go back to your home, to your wife and parents, and eat good food, this state of mind may degenerate; it will change. You will once again develop attachment to material things – to home, family and comfort, wife and children. You will feel disgust when things are dirty and feel happy when things are clean. If someone speaks kindly or rudely you will develop liking and disliking. If you discover that your mind has changed in this way, the feelings that will arise are not good. Listen to me: keep this mind, which remains unattached to material things and go on a pilgrimage to Nepal for one or two years. Then you will successfully accomplish the Dharma. Even if you were unable to reach Nepal itself, it would be as if you had gone on pilgrimage anyway. Even if you were only able to take three steps and then die, by maintaining this state of mind you would have been successful in your practice."

I recovered from my surprise after a moment. "I am uncertain about two years," I said. "I don't know the language or the region, but in keeping with your instructions I will go for one year."

Pilgrimage to Nepal

While continuing to receive teachings from my lama, I stayed in a cave once inhabited by the great female Tibetan saint Machik Labdron, so that I could put these teachings into practice. I had stayed in this cave on many occasions over the years, and this time there were about thirteen lay practitioners and nuns who had gathered there for meditation.

Because Naptra Rinpoche had requested that I go to Nepal, I wanted to set out on my journey as soon as possible, but I had very little barley flour left for the journey. One day I decided to invite all my fellow practitioner friends for a Tsok, or sacred feast offering. Whatever food I had, I offered in the ceremony, including my small supply of flour.

Normally, ascetic practitioners are careful with their food supplies. The nuns noted my actions. "He has completely changed," they said, "and he is acting completely crazy."

One old nun even said, "He must not be well; he must have gone insane."

Another nun, Kalsang, was bold enough to ask me about this directly. "You have offered all the food you have for the ceremony," she said. "Haven't you become a little bit mad?"

"I'm not mad," I replied jokingly. "But I do feel a little crazy, like I'm about to go wild."

After three days I again called my friends back to the cave. This time I asked them to take all of my belongings, my tables, clay pots, blankets – everything. "I'm going to Nepal and I don't know whether I will return. Except for my copper pots, which I'll need if I come back, would you please take everything?"

They were initially shy about this, but then they complied, gradually removing all my possessions from the cave.

After some time, one of the lamas at the cave came to me and expressed his concerns for me. "I heard that you gave everything away to the others. Have you gone mad?"

"I'm not crazy," I replied. "I'm just going on a pilgrimage."

He paused and then asked me, "But to whom did you give your good lambskin coat?"

"I kept it for myself as a blanket," I answered.

He looked at me, and then said, "Sell it to me."

Because I knew that this lama had a good drum and ritual trumpet from the Kham region of Tibet, used by his own guru, I made him a proposal. "If you give me your damaru and kangling, I will give you my lambskin coat – and I can then start off on my pilgrimage." He had fallen in love with the coat, but he also wanted my two leather bags, which I used to carry flour. "You can take these, too," I told him.

I felt really happy about getting his damaru and kangling. Having given everything to my close friends, there was nothing left except my wood-framed backpack.

About this same time, I met a great Dzokchen practitioner named Kushu Pema, from Langkor. He was a great yogi with long dreadlocks tied up around his head. He gave me the transmission for Machik Lapdron's meditation tradition called "Shije kyi Kor." I was surprised that he read the texts at a constant pace, never stopping to eat or even stretch his legs.

The year was 1958. I had a strong wish at the time to see my wife and grandfather just one more time before I left on my pilgrimage to Nepal.

My wife, Kalsang Drolma, had been staying near a cave called Jashu, practicing Dharma there. I learned that she was pregnant again. Little did I know that this was the last time I would ever see her, and I wouldn't meet my son until he was 21 years old. His name would be Tsering Dundrup.

I also wanted to visit Grandfather Penakpa, with whom I had always been close. When I traveled there and found him, he was sleeping in the field where the barley was winnowed and separated. "Where are you going?" he asked me.

"I'm just going to Nyalam, not really very far." I didn't tell him about giving my possessions away, or about the long pilgrimage ahead. As my grandfather and I spoke there in the barley field, my unkind stepmother watched us from a room on the top floor of the house. She wondered about who was down there, and when she found out that it was me, she went and hid herself!

My grandfather offered his help. "If you are just going to Langkor," he said, "you don't need to carry your bag on your back. You can borrow one of my horses." But, because he didn't have a horse available for loan at the time, he brought me a white ox instead.

"Take this ox up to Langkor," he told me.

"But if I take this ox, will it be able to return home?"

"Well, of course," he said. "This ox is very obedient; it knows the road very well. Just chase it down to the river, and it will find its way back with no problem."

Before I left there, I prayed that I would see my grandfather again. I didn't think much about my stepmother or my father. I offered my grandfather a portion of meat, and then I started off on my journey.

Just before I reached Langkor, I unloaded my pack from the ox. I led it down to the river. Just as my grandfather had said, the ox headed off straight toward home. I still had my faithful sheep as a companion, and though my grandfather's village had a flock of almost a thousand sheep, I had decided to not leave him there; in this village they regularly slaughtered sheep.

Fortunately, during my earlier journey, I had visited the Matze family in the village of Shelkar. Here they kept many sheep, but they did not kill them. This town, in the district of Tingri, had received its name directly from Padampa Sangye according to the following legend:

A long time ago, when Dampa Sangye was searching for the stone that the Buddha had thrown, he noticed a spot of land that wasn't covered by snow. Approaching a family who lived there, he said, "I'm on a pilgrimage and am feeling very cold. Could you give me something warm to drink?"

The mother of the house had two kettles of tea on. She offered Dampa the kettle that was almost empty, and when she poured the tea, it filled only half his cup. Just then the sun came in through the window, and the light fell on this portion.

"What is your family's name?" asked Dampa.

"Champa," said the mother.

"Your tea did not fill up my cup, so your family lineage will not enjoy wealth. But because the sun fell on the cup, your lineage will be long. Because the sun rose as you poured the tea, you will be called Shelkar, or white crystal."

I explained this to these gentle people. "My grandfather's village slaughters sheep, and I know that your village does not do this. This particular sheep has accompanied me on my sacred pilgrimage to one hundred eight cemeteries. I would like to save his life. Therefore, I would like to leave him with you. You can shear his wool, and you may use him for your work. When he dies, you can throw his corpse in the river. He will be no problem to you." They promised to take care of my sheep, and I went on my way.

Some five years later, while I was staying in a Sherpa village, I had a dream about that sheep, and I thought that he must have died. I didn't have the necessary supplies to do a ritual feast at the time, so I just offered some butter lamps and did prayers for his benefit.

Friends on the Path

I reached the village of Langkor at mid-afternoon. I had known that if I told my mother or sisters about my going to Nepal, they would have cried. So I dared not go into the village, and I stayed in a stone sheep barn at the edge of the village. At dusk, I walked to the Mani temple nearby, set my bags down in the courtyard, and requested the treasurer's permission to see the statue of Padampa Sangye. I thought that this might be the very last time I would see this holy statue, so I prayed before it and circumambulated three times before I left there.

As I walked on into the night, I saw three people together on the darkening road; I wondered about where they were traveling – whether they might be going in the same direction as I was.. One of them wore a hat typical of what monks wore. They appeared to be genuine practitioners. We came closer on the road and I asked, "Where are you from?"

"We are from Sutso village, which is just below Naptra Rinpoche's monastery."

"And whose family are you from?" I asked.

"I am Losang," said the monk. He was, it turned out, an old dharma acquaintance of mine. In fact, we had previously received a Chöd initiation together. They were also going towards Nyalam.

"Is there any place to stay the night?" they asked me.

"It's difficult," I said. "I haven't yet found a place to stay. I'm just planning to stay in the Mani temple courtyard."

Losang, his wife Konchog, and their friend Ani Timok stayed with me that night. They had brought some firewood, so we made tea and a boiled noodle soup. We decided to travel together from that point, which gave me the opportunity to teach them some Chöd practices along the way.

One evening along the way, we talked about the high pass that we would have to cross over the next day. Because they were bringing wool blankets and a large piece of meat to sell in Nepal, their backpacks were very heavy. I suggested we rent two pack animals from my cousin Namkha, who lived nearby. This would make the crossing much easier.

We arrived at Namkha's house about midnight, and we knocked on his door. He responded immediately and invited us inside. "But we don't need to come in," we said. "We just want to hire two pack animals from you to help us cross the high pass. We are leaving quite early in the morning." Namkha quickly brought us two yaks; our bags were soon loaded and we continued with him toward the pass, now carrying only our walking sticks.

That next day we crossed the pass and stayed in the valley on the other side. When the sun rose, we made tea and I paid my cousin for the stock rental with a pair of well-made Tibetan boots. He headed back toward home, and we continued towards Nyalam. Still, though, Losang had a very heavy pack to carry, so I suggested that to lighten our load, we should offer some of our things in a ritual when we reached Milarepa's cave. They agreed, but just as we were making the offerings, they began to have doubts, saying, "If we finish all our barley flour, how will we eat?"

"We can go beg for food," I replied. "We will have enough to eat." But when I said this, they just laughed. None of them had any experience in asking for alms!

While we were performing the ceremony, monks from a nearby monastery came by and asked us what kind of ritual we were doing. We told them that it was the Chöd offering practice. "Since we are Gelugpas," they said, "you are not allowed to play drums or bells inside our monastery compound. But just below this cave is a house. There you can perform your Chöd." We were allowed inside the house, which had a large garden, and there we stayed to offer our ritual.

We finally arrived at the town of Nyalam Tsongdu. Because it was by now autumn, there were many people bringing sheep to sell to the Nepalese for slaughter. I didn't want to see all this killing, so I didn't stay. "Let's leave for Nepal as soon as we can," I said to my friends.

"It will be too hot down there if we leave now," protested Losang. But this wasn't the real reason he didn't want to go. He was a skilled tailor and was being paid very well for his services here. His wife could also weave aprons and other fabric. Both of them had become quite busy with their work. I told them that I was going to leave on my own, but they refused to let me go. "You don't know which road to take," they insisted. "We will guide you there later."

"As long as you're staying here," I asked them, "please take me to a cave where I can stay and practice."

A friend of Losang's, who sold yogurt and firewood, was from a mountain village not far from town. She knew the area well. "There are many places to stay," she said. "Just up there is a spot called Pulok. Farther above that is a monastery called Pelay, and beyond the monastery is a mountain with many caves. You can stay up there, but you will need courage, because there are strange noises at night. But if you are really interested I will show you the cave."

And so I went with this woman to find a place of solitude.

The Cave of Prophecy

This woman first took me to her small house. Her mother suffered from a foot ailment, and she asked if I could perform a healing ceremony for her. I said I would try to help, and that night I practiced Chöd, chasing away all the negative spirits in that place. The next day, she took me to a cave that was situated above some beautiful pastures and a small nunnery called Pelay.

"In this cave you will hear noises during the night," she said. "So don't be surprised. If you need food we will offer it to you."

I stayed there for two months. People started coming to me to ask for divinations and other kinds of help. I decided to practice a deity meditation called Palden Lhamo, and I made offerings to her, as she is very important for certain kinds of divinatory work. In order to perform Palden Lhamo prophecy, one needs to have an image of her, along with a pair of dice and a mirror. I didn't have a painting, so I set out to borrow one from the nunnery below.

Between my cave and the nunnery lived an old man called Nepo Tang Gelong, who was on retreat. I went down to ask him if he had a Palden Lhamo painting that I could borrow for several days. Meanwhile, though, the nuns had seen Lhamo Tsering, the woman who had shown me this cave, bringing me food and other offerings. They reported this to the Gelong, who said to me jokingly, "You don't need a painting of Palden Lhamo, you have Lhamo Tsering coming to you every day."

"Who told you that?" I asked.

"The nuns told me that they see her going there every day," he replied.

"That's right. She showed me the cave and offered to bring me food if I didn't have any."

The Gelong laughed and offered me rice and good tea. "I don't have any Palden Lhamo paintings, but the nunnery below has many. You can go there to find one."

So I went to the nunnery, and I asked for permission to visit the main shrine room. The two nuns in charge showed me in, and there I found three paintings of Palden Lhamo. "May I borrow this small one for a month in order to do my practice?" I asked them.

The two nuns, who were quite young, said no. "We don't know where you are from. If you leave with the scroll, how will we be able to find you? It's not possible. And the older nuns are very difficult. If we do something positive, they will not praise us. If we do something wrong, they will scream at us. They say neither please nor thank you! They would be angry if we lent you that painting."

One of those nuns is now in Dharamsala. And the other is now my consort. Her name is Tashi Lhamo, which means Auspicious Goddess.

So I did the practice there without any Thanka paintings for one month. After that, I told Lhamo Tsering that I should return to the village to meet my friends. She requested that I stay at her home for two days before leaving. After reading religious texts there for two days, Dorje Phuntsok, the father of the wealthy Shungpa family, asked if I would help read the Prajnaparamita in 100,000 verses in his home with two other monks. The annual reading of holy texts is traditionally done to bring good luck to the household.

Dorje Phuntsok stayed and listened while the monks and I read the texts, and then he had his wife provide me with a silver cup holder. He said, "This monk deserves to drink from a vessel of this kind." Indeed, I was a skilled text reader during this period of my youth. We recited the text for seven days, and while reading I came to a deep understanding of the perfection of wisdom and of the concept of shunyata, or emptiness.

My patron then had another request. Normally, during harvest, farmers take the yaks out to stomp on the barley, but if snow falls then, it will completely destroy the crop. Dorje Phuntsok explained, "Tomorrow I am going to separate the stalks from the barley with my ten yaks. Can you please prevent snow from falling tonight?"

I offered incense and prayers three times and that night it did not snow. Perhaps it was because of my prayers, or perhaps it was just the weather! In any case, Dorje became convinced that I was able to control the elements. "After you return from Kathmandu, you are welcome to stay here. I have another cave just above the one where you stayed. I will offer you food and clothing or whatever else you need. Please come back!"

His wife then spoke to me. "The people of Nyalam village are unpredictable. At first they might support you, but there is no promise of that. Though Dorje offered you all you need while you stay, we can in reality give you only butter and barley from our own land. We might not be able to supply you with meat and rice; those come from the village."

Before I left for Kathmandu, as a final token of gratitude, Dorje offered me tea, flour, and butter. He repaired my worn out shoes and treated me with great kindness.

Healings on the Road to Kathmandu

When I returned to the market and met my friends, they were completely absorbed in their work. Well paid and well fed, they were no longer interested in leaving. As it happened, I met a couple from my village who were also going to Kathmandu, and so we decided to walk together. Starting out, we first came to Chogsham, where we stayed with a family in a wooden house. They had a son who had been quite ill for a long time; he was in severe pain when we arrived. Everyone believed that he was dying, and the family asked me to do a divination and help their ailing son. "I don't know about divination," I replied, "but I can perform Chöd." And so that night I did my practice. All the doors were shut, but just as I finished the ritual, the main door slammed open with a loud "bang." Everyone was startled. "It is not a problem," I said. "The demon has fled the house."

"Is it true?" they asked.

"Yes, it is true; the demon who was harming your son has gone." Then we all retired for the night.

The next morning the father came to me with a bucket of corn flour and rice. "My son has recovered completely," he said. "Thank you very much." I took some provisions for myself and gave the rest to my travel companions.

Next we reached a market called Dram on the other side of the border. The year must have been 1958. In Dram I stayed in the house of a Sherpa family. The house had a large area with a kitchen and bedroom, which the family rented to travelers. The wife had a baby of about ten months old. "Two sons have passed away before reaching their first year," they . "We expect this child to die also. One lama told us that if we offered 100,000 ritual cakes or tormas, our son would survive, and so now I offer these cakes each morning. Because you know this practice, can you help us to do 100,000 offerings for our son?"

I agreed to help, but when they showed me the kitchen where I was to offer these tormas, I saw that it was a place that many travelers had passed through. They ate, drank rice beer, got drunk, and sometimes fought. I explained to the man that it was not possible to offer ritual cakes there, because all the previous activity would be too disruptive to the offerings. Was there somewhere more remote that I could go?

Yes, he said, indeed there was, and so we set out the next day to find a suitable place for practice.

We reached the side of the mountain, where there was a monastery and a few caves, but there were many people living in this area. Higher up we found a three-walled sheltered cave in a quiet place, with patches of soft grass. "This is perfect!" I said. "I am going to stay here."

"Bears and snow leopards may come," the man warned. "And your shelter doesn't have a door. It is not safe for you."

"I have a small tent I can use as a door. If a bear or leopard comes, I will blow my thighbone trumpet." Still, the Sherpa was not convinced. I reassured him that it wasn't going to be a problem and reaffirmed my decision to stay. The next morning we carried supplies up to my shelter on the mountain. After four days, the man came to check on how I was doing. He opened my tent door with his knife drawn, just in case there was a wild animal feasting on me. "I'm still here," I said. "Please, won't you come in?" He shyly put his knife away. After two or three more visits, he became less worried that I would be eaten by wild beasts, and he was content to check on me only every ten days or so.

I was well settled in my cave dwelling, when one day my matchsticks ran out and I was not able to make a fire. I couldn't make tea, so I had to eat just raw flour and water. Three days later, I heard the sound of Tibetans approaching. They opened the tent door and I beheld a monk and a woman wearing an apron and carrying a thermos. At first I thought they might be demons, but as they approached they said, "Oh, lama is here, lama is here." I invited them inside and asked them to sit.

"Where are you from?" they inquired.

"I'm from Tingri."

"Are you a monk from Tsipri?" the woman asked.

"No. My lama is Naptra Rinpoche."

"I am from Tsipri," she said, "and a disciple of Tripon Rinpoche. Yesterday we met a Sherpa man who said he was supplying food to a lama living up here. We thought you must be a disciple of Tripon Rinpoche, for who else would stay in such a remote place? This is why I came to see you. But even though you are from Naptra Rinpoche, it doesn't really matter. Please have some tea." They had three matchsticks with them and I was finally able to make a fire.

"Your tea was excellent but your matchsticks were even more wonderful," I joked. The monk, who was a Geshe, questioned me about my background and I told him that I was from the Penakpa family.

"Oh, Penakpa was my sponsor. Are you the monk from Shelkar Chöde monastery?"

"No," I replied; I wished to avoid talking about my time as an official.

But I was surprised when he said, "If you are not the monk from Shelkar Chöde then you must be black-face lama!" The Geshe even knew the nickname from my youth! Then he stood up and offered me three prostrations. "You were a good boy when you were small, but now you are a great practitioner. I have done many pujas in your home and I knew your whole family. You shouldn't stay here. You don't even have any rugs to put on the ground, and you may become sick. I will make a good place for you to stay near the monastery."

The offer was appealing, but I declined. "I have to offer 100,000 ritual cakes. When I finish, I will come down." After five days I finished the practice and proceeded to the Geshe's home.

The Geshe lived in a large house. He showed me another small house where he said I could stay, but it didn't look very safe – the roof appeared ready to fall in. On a distant hill I spotted some prayer flags and benches, and I told him I would rather stay up there. "Why would you stay there? That's where Sherpas do their pujas. Don't you feel afraid to stay in such a place?"

"I have stayed in such sacred places many times. I'm not frightened." So I walked to the place, and I put my tent up in the midst of the log benches. The Geshe brought me a pot for cooking, some meat, and some long-haired yak wool blankets, which I used as rugs. He visited me at night and we drank rice beer together. I stayed there for five days, but then I developed an ache in my legs. Maybe it was because, as the Geshe suggested, I had neglected to use a carpet for such a long time. The pain became so intense that I had to use walking sticks to move around.

The Geshe recommended I go to Tatopani, where the hot springs might help my condition. The Geshe had a wife who helped me carry my baggage, and we walked to Tatopani together. I went to a big guesthouse with two floors, but because I had so much knee pain, I stayed on the ground floor. There were also two Nepalese staying there, one an old man with many wounds. Thinking back, I would now say that he must have had leprosy. He and I shared the same room. We became good friends and shared our food. I blew mantras on his wounds and we washed together in the hot springs. After fifteen days he mostly recovered, and he went home. I stayed there for a further month, until I too was cured.

Visions and Shamans

Just below Tatopani was a wide river with no bridge. To ferry people to the other side, a rope was tied between two trees, with a basket suspended from the rope across the river. Riding across in this device cost twelve cents. After safely getting to the other side, I met several Tibetans. When I asked where they were going, they all replied, "We're going back to Tibet." We parted ways and, carrying my backpack and walking stick, I continued to walk alone by the riverside, headed toward Kathmandu. But knowing that my fellow Tibetans were traveling north, back to Tibet, I felt a little sad. I stopped, found a large boulder, and just sat for a while and meditated on Guru Rinpoche. Soon, a large cloud above a distant mountain took on the appearance of Guru Rinpoche himself, clear and vivid. He wore blue robes and a lotus hat, and he held a holy man's staff in his left hand. With his right hand he indicated the way I should travel. I then felt very happy and comforted.

I pushed myself along the road. When I reached a particular high pass, I saw some distant white houses surrounded by a green field. Just before reaching this village I met an old woman with white hair and a red dress, carrying a basket of grass on her back.

"Where are you going?" she asked in Sherpa dialect.

"I have no idea, and I don't have anywhere to stay. Do you know a place I can rest tonight?"

"Yes, of course" she said warmly. I followed her to her house, small quarters facing a triangular-shaped courtyard, where two cows were tied to a post. The roof was made of slate and inside was a grass mattress and some firewood laid next to a stone hearth. Seeing this mattress and hearth made me very happy. "Will this do?" she asked.

"Yes, I like it very much!" I took off my backpack and lay down exhausted on the mattress.

After some time, the old woman brought me a plate of corn dough and a bowl of yogurt, telling me, "If you don't have any other place, you can stay here as long as you want. I will offer you food."

"I will stay for a little while," I said, "and then I'll go on to Kathmandu. Later I will return." I stayed and practiced for a full month. I felt very happy with the Nepalese landscape and houses. It all seemed so enchanting and beautiful.

I then journeyed on to Kathmandu, along with two Tibetans I had met. The first place we reached was Namo Buddha, a sacred place for Buddhists. There I performed a Chöd offering. Afterwards, a Tamang lama asked me where I had learned my Chöd practice. "You practice exactly like my lama Surkang in Tingri. Because you know this practice, I will let you stay here with me." I stayed for one week and promised to visit him again.

Next, I reached Boudhanath, the place of the Great Stupa. Here I stayed for one month with an old man who painted wall hangings and also took care of the stupa. He was kind enough to offer me food during my stay. From Boudha I walked to Jawalakhel and stayed in a guesthouse next to the zoo.

I then proceeded to Pharping, where I stayed in a guesthouse next to a small lake. Some Nepalese people came to the temple in the early morning to do pujas or ceremonies, singing and playing drums and bells. There was also an old man who lived there who owned the only restaurant in the village. He sold meat and rice beer, and he regularly visited the Vajrayogini temple on the hill. At the time, no monasteries had yet been built; in fact, there was only the one guesthouse. Other than two or three other houses and a small bazaar, Pharping was virtually empty. In the morning, there were no sounds other than the songs of birds and the rippling water of the lake. It was very peaceful and I stayed in this idyllic Pharping for one month.

One night I did Chöd in the rocky caves above the temple. At around eleven o'clock a tiger revealed itself from the bushes. It was scratching the ground and growling loudly. I blew my thighbone trumpet and it jumped down from the caves to the stream below.

The next day I decided to wander down through the forest to have a look around. As I walked through the trees, I saw a glowing red light through the branches. As I got closer, I realized that it was actually a small fire. Next to a large tree and the glowing embers was a woman lying on a patch of grass. She was naked and covered with ashes. Around her neck were prayer beads. A walking stick lay beside her on the ground, and both she and the fire were encircled by a red rope. This wandering yogini, a female meditation master, spoke to me in Nepalese. "Whatever you do, please don't come within the rope." I thought she must be a manifestation of Vajrayogini or Dorje Phagmo and I became joyful.

"Where do you come from?" she asked.

"I have come from Tibet. But what are you doing here?"

"I'm trying to bring rain."

"Last night there was a big noise. What was that?"

"It was the sound of a tiger," she said. "Were you afraid?"

"Yes, I was."

"Why be scared? You stayed in the protection of the rocky caves. I stayed only in the shelter of a large tree in the jungle, yet I had no fear."

Later some Nepalese came to bring her fruits. She put on some red clothes and left with them. That night it rained very heavily.

I found out later she had also received teachings from my lama, Naptra Rinpoche, when he visited Nepal. Because she could bring rain, she was given a position by the king of Nepal and could enter the palace at any time. She sought permission from the government to build monasteries; she was called "Ama Devi." Later I saw her in a photograph with the king, wearing her long hair like Shiva, holding a ritual object in her right hand and a long life vase in her left.

Sickness and Recovery

After a month by the lake I went up to Asura Cave, where Guru Rinpoche had once meditated on the Vajrakilaya Tantra. At the time, the trail was hardly visible. Just in front of the cave were some bricks piled up for a hearth; fresh water had to be carried up from a spring below. A short, old Tamang lama who spoke Tibetan lived in a red house just below the cave. When pilgrims came, he sold them butter lamps for two rupees. He told me where I could beg for alms. "If you go this way, you might get rice. If you go that way, you might get corn." I spent one month here doing practice. When it was time to move on, he showed me the trail that led to Rikeswor, another holy place for Guru Rinpoche.

On the way to Rikeswor, on a high mountain pass, I stayed in a barn with animal pastures all around. That night I heard a tiger roaring close by, and I remembered Ama Devi. From here I walked down to the valley and stayed by the riverside. Though there were many houses scattered about, this place was very quiet. Continuing on, I stayed on a hill slope where the villagers helped me find the way to Rikeswor. They warned me, "It is very remote and there are no places to obtain food or shelter. If you beg there, you will get only red rice and corn beer."

When I arrived at Rikeswor, I stayed in a three-walled shelter, which had a broken white Guru Rinpoche statue inside. At this point, I started to become very ill, and I didn't know why. My feet and face became swollen, and people said my complexion was yellow. It might have been because I was living on tsampa and rice and wasn't eating any meat. One day, an old Tamang lady gave me a chicken, which I ate, but still I did not recover. A Tamang lama suggested I go to Swayambhu and make buffalo meat soup as a remedy for this condition. I started walking, but could only move very slowly. From Rikeswor it took me a full five days to reach Swayambhu.

In Swayambhu, I stayed in a guesthouse – it is still there, these many years later. Nearby, the butchers cut up water buffalo. They used to throw the legs away, so I collected these and put them in some clay pots. I would wash the legs, boil them for a whole day, and eat this soup at night. Though otherwise tough and inedible, when simmered for a whole day, this meat becomes very delicious. I begged for alms and received as much rice, flour, and beer as I needed. I recovered very well after a month on this regimen and was once again able to circumambulate the stupa and practice Chöd. I was then able to return to Boudha, and I lived in a different place there. There was plenty of firewood in those days, and donkeys were commonly seen on the streets.

I met two Tibetans from Nyalam who came to sell sheep in Nepal. We were happy to see each other, as there were no other Tibetans around. One was named Tashi Topgye, the other Tenzin Norbu. Tenzin, the older one, had many stories he liked to tell. "If you pray to the stupa for anything, you will receive it. If you want children you will get children, and if you pray for wealth you will obtain wealth." They gave me flour and meat from Tibet, as well as tea and some money. Their business must have been good, because they sponsored the repainting of the stupa and put up new prayer flags. "Come with us back to our village," they asked. "We don't have any lama." Even in Boudha at that time, there was only one lama, named Gya Lama. He had the only monastery there, and he was highly respected. If you asked for a blessing he would just recite one Guru Rinpoche mantra.

I told these elderly and prosperous Tibetans, "I can't go until one year is finished here, according to my lama's specific instructions."

The Drunken Lama

After a month in Boudha, I went to Sankhu, where there is an ancient and holy Vajrayogini temple. But situated just below the temple was a place for animal sacrifice. Though the Ganesh statue there was very white, the ground below was completely red with blood. Because this upset me very much, the people in the guesthouse where I stayed suggested that I should stay in the caves far above. I stayed for twelve days and then set out for my return to Tatopani and the border.

Again I had to cross a wide river, but this time there was a boat to ferry people across. People sat in single file in this long wooden boat, and though this seemed safer than the rope and harness previously used, the boat suddenly capsized as we neared the shore. I couldn't swim, but fortunately my belt had become caught on a nail in the boat, and it took me to the other side where I immediately grabbed onto a tree. I was safe, but all my things had fallen in. The Nepalese people were able to swim, and they recovered my baggage, but my flour and drum were soaked. I stayed by the riverbank to dry my belongings, spreading them out beneath a tree, while the other people continued on.

Both sadness and happiness filled my heart then. All my clothes and food were wet. I just lay there naked. Just then two old Tamang women and their children appeared. "You're completely naked!" they cried. "Are you crazy?"

"No, I'm not crazy. My boat capsized and all my possessions fell into the river. I'm just drying my clothes."

"Oh, are you cold?"

"Yes."

"Would you like some liquor?"

"Yes, actually, I would."

I held up my wooden bowl and she filled it from her flask. I drank the liquor slowly, and I didn't notice that I was becoming drunk. The melancholy feeling drifted away, my body warmed up, and I began to sing and dance. From the hilltops some Nepalese people watched my naked dancing in amusement.

That night, as I slept under the tree without any cover – because of my wet blankets – I had a very disturbing dream. A tall black woman stood in front of me, her face resembling the woman who had given me the liquor. In my hand was a two-foot long sword, very bright and shining in all directions. I wondered how I had obtained this sword. But the woman told me, "The sword is to cut your head off. It would be very good if you did this."

"But won't I die if I cut off my own head?" I asked.

"You won't die, you won't get sick, and you won't even get hurt." So I held my head and cut through it; it sliced like butter.

"Cut one more time," she ordered. I cut once more above where I had just cut. In the dream I didn't die, nor did I feel hurt or sick, just as she had said.

When I awoke, I thought this woman was a bad woman, and that I had encountered a serious obstacle. Many doubts arose in me. I checked my body and didn't find any signs of sickness, so I put on my backpack and resumed my journey back toward Tibet. Later, when I stopped to rest and began to make tea, I met a Geshe from Sera, a large Gelugpa monastery. He said he was on pilgrimage to Kathmandu, and I consulted him about my dream. "You shouldn't be afraid," he said. "It was a very auspicious dream. The appearance of Dorje Phagmo in the dream shows you are able to cut through your ego. You should keep this secret." The Geshe advised me very well.

I reached Barrabes, where a Newari man offered me much rice. I took this rice to the old Sherpa woman who had given me a room a year earlier when I had first come from Tibet. Since then nearly a year had passed, and she was happy to see me again. The old woman had three sons, all married, and she invited me to join her whole family for a hot spring bath at Tatopani. But without my knowledge, they bought a live chicken, and I saw them butcher it.

"Why did you kill the chicken!?" I exclaimed.

"When we take a hot spring bath, we kill a chicken to help remove difficult emotions."

Maybe I was still drunk on the liquor, but I cried right there in front of her. I felt very bad being with people who would buy and then kill animals. They asked me why I was crying. "It's all right to buy meat," I said, "but to buy a live chicken and kill it is really terrible. I don't like killing, and now I feel like I'm staying with murderers." They were saddened by this, and they stopped killing chickens.

No Return

One year and two months had passed since I left Tibet. It was time to begin my journey back, but soon after I set out for home, I met a monk with a twisted mouth. "The situation in Tibet is not good at all," he told me. "The Chinese have invaded, and the Dalai lama has fled to India. It is not wise to go back now." This was the first news I had heard about my homeland since my departure. I was in shock. Now, instead of traveling to the border, I had to return to my Sherpa family. Her sons advised me not to go anywhere, and offered to let me stay with them for a while.

In the hills above Kathmandu was a large village called Tang Shing, and on the other side of the valley was the village of Marme. Fifteen or twenty monks usually participated in Nyingma rituals for these villages. But when someone died in Tang Shing village, four or five Sherpa lamas would get together to lead the pujas, and the Sherpa people themselves would perform a ritual and give alms.

Because I could read well, I agreed to help them. They asked me to perform Chöd, and when I finished the lamas were very happy and appreciated me very much. "You don't have a father, a mother, a wife, or children," they said. "In our texts it is prophesied that a son without a father and mother who works to help other people is a reincarnated lama who came to the world to benefit beings. You must be this lama. You don't need to ask for alms anymore. We will provide you with your food from now on."

Accordingly, when the corn was harvested, the Tang Shing villagers would offer me about eighty barrels. The Marme villagers offered me ninety barrels. Each year, it took eight or nine porters to carry it all. I didn't have any place to store these grains, so I placed them in big round bamboo baskets and gave away barrels of the corn to the poor Sherpa villagers.

Meanwhile, no matter which way I contrived to return to Tibet, it increasingly seemed impossible. More and more people were leaving Tibet all the time, and the news was getting worse. Finally the border was closed off completely. There was no longer any chance of returning home.

I stayed in the village with the Sherpa family for a total of five years after that. During my stay, they were somewhat poor, but they did own two cows. I shared the corn I had, and I did a ceremony for them to "hook in" prosperity and good fortune. And later they did become quite rich. During my stay, I also renovated a stupa that stood above the road, so people could walk underneath it and receive blessings.

Among the many Tibetans fleeing their own country, four Khampas stayed in the village. One was an old man who was good at inscribing mantras in stone. I put him to work, giving him corn to inscribe mantras. He made Mani and Vajra Guru mantras and Long Life prayers. I created a small Mani wall with his stones and put up a large prayer flag. Gradually, seven more Tibetan families came to live there. They would come to buy corn from me, which at the time was one rupee for three kilograms (more than six pounds) of corn. Yet one porter carrying corn was paid ten rupees! And when the harvest was good, the price of corn was only one half rupee per kilogram.

Although many Tibetans were escaping, I didn't meet anyone from my area of Tingri, so I decided to visit Kathmandu once again. I found that in Boudha there were already many Tibetans. A refugee camp had started up in Jawalakhel, where they were spinning and weaving carpets in a makeshift tin shantytown. People lived in small thatched houses with bamboo walls; they collected firewood from the nearby mountains. At three in the morning a man would cry, "Let's get wood!" Some people would go out and collect firewood. By ten they would come back with their baskets full. They used to bring me a little of their wood, and in return I would perform ceremonies for them.

I rented a small room in a Nepalese style house from a Brahmin family; the rent was only three rupees a month! In the other room was a policeman with a wife and son. I stayed for one winter season, and then I planned to go back to the Sherpa village. But before I could leave, the Tibetans all implored me, "Don't stay in a Nepalese village so far away! Stay with the Tibetans in the camp. If you die in that village, there won't be anybody to take care of us." So I stayed in Kathmandu a while longer.

Lama Wangdu, Nepal 1958. Age 22

Naptra Rinpoche, Pre-1957, colorized.

Lama Wangdu, 2007 performing Chöd ritual dance

Lama Wangdu, circa 1980 performing Chöd at Maratika cave, Nepal

Lama Wangdu, circa 2000 Mt. Hood, OR

His Holiness the Dalai Lama, and Lama Wangdu. Circa 2000. Lama Wangdu visited His Holiness the Dalai Lama on several occasions where the preservation of Padampa's lineage was discussed.

Pilgrimage in India

From the many Tibetan refugees, I soon heard news that His Holiness the Dalai Lama was in Dharamsala, in northern India. I very much wanted to visit him, and I began planning a pilgrimage. But at that time very few Tibetans knew Hindi, the language of India. Of three families who invited me to go to India with them, only one man among them could speak a little Hindi, so I decided to go with his group. I had been staying in Boudha with a Tibetan family from Nyalam village for some time, and they assured me that I didn't need to take anything with me for the journey – no blankets, no food, nothing. "The Dalai Lama has already arrived in India," they said. "You don't need to pay for the train. You don't need to pay for food. Just bring one mug, some beaten rice, and a small blanket. This is enough." I listened to their advice, and believed that I didn't need to ask the other individuals or families in the area about this.

The next day, though, when I met the other families traveling to India they remarked on my lack of belongings. "You don't even have a pot to carry!"

I repeated to them what the Nyalam family had told me. "But nobody will give you anything free," they said. But by then it was too late – we were already on the road. In the truck along with me was the Hindi-speaking gentleman, his mother, and a brother who was a monk. None of us had experienced traveling by motor before, and everyone was carsick, throwing up into their cooking pots.

The old woman in our truck lamented, "Why did I come here?"

I consoled her: "Because we are going on pilgrimage, saying this will only accumulate non-virtue."

When we stopped and finally got down from the truck, they had to boil tea in those same pots! I quietly ate my beaten rice and tea. However, the next morning I felt nauseated and had sores on my face; then I got heat sickness. When we reached Lucknow to catch our train, I was so ill that I fell asleep right on the platform. An Indian man woke me and asked me to accompany him. I asked my Hindi-speaking Tibetan friend, "What does this man have in mind?"

"He said he would like to take you to a good health clinic." So I let him lead me to a hospital near the train station. The doctor gave me a complete checkup, and prescribed some pills and ointment, but didn't ask for any payment at all. After taking this medicine, I made a speedy recovery.

We arrived in Dharamsala at the end of the month, two weeks before Losar, the Tibetan New Year. Because there were no houses in the area, we simply stayed under a tree. We also learned that His

Holiness gave audiences only on Wednesdays and Saturdays. My Tibetan friends, after having two such audiences, decided to go back to Nepal. They said they didn't have time to go on further pilgrimage in India; they needed to be home to plant their crop of potatoes. I asked the one monk in our group, "Because we are both religious practitioners, wouldn't it be good to go on pilgrimage together? We have already come to India, and it would be a shame not to visit the holy places of the Buddha. Let them go back; we can go visit the sacred sites together."

"Oh, there is no way I could go with you," he replied. Looking at me very seriously, he said, "Indian people take you and hang you up by your feet. Then they squeeze you to make oil. I am too scared to go. I will go back to Nepal." So the next day every single one of them returned home. To this day I still sometimes tease this man about what he said that day, which always brings him laughter.

Dharamsala Experiences

I was now alone in Dharamsala without even my cooking pots; I had just my cup for food and tea. I carried my blanket and bag to a guesthouse and asked the old Tibetan who owned it if I could stay there. "It's not possible," he said. I went a little farther up the hill, where I found an aged monk. "I don't have any pots to cook with. May I join you?" I asked.

"Okay, you can stay," he replied simply. The venerable monk, whose only possessions were some worn blankets, a few pieces of luggage and some old pots, said he was from Yangpachen, a Gelugpa monastery. He slept on a hammock placed across a wooden beam. "You don't have rugs or padding," he said. "I have something to put on the floor, so why don't you sleep on the hammock." He and I soon became friends and shared our food and conversation.

The next day was Losar. All the Tibetans made fried cookies in their small pots, but my monk friend and I didn't have any oil to fry with. He told me, "Please do a wealth enhancing puja and I will go out to beg for alms. Soon we will have more cookies than the others." I put tea and rice in a copper butter pot and made a prayer to White Ganesh. The monk went off to beg for alms, carrying his bag on his shoulder and twirling his damaru drum. He left early in the morning, but returned after only a few hours. I thought something must be wrong, but his bag was already completely filled with cookies and boiled rice! We ate well that day and had enough food to set aside for a while.

On the third day after Losar, the King of Ladakh had an audience with His Holiness. My monk friend had a clever thought. "Would you like to have His Holiness speak to you?"

"Yes, I would love that," I said. So we joined in line with the Ladakhi workmen who were carrying the statues and thangkas that their king was offering to His Holiness. I asked one man, "What is that text you're carrying?"

"This text is the Lam Rim," he told us, as my friend and I made our way closer to His Holiness.

When we arrived, His Holiness was standing, giving his blessings to each offering. All the thangkas and statues were then put aside. Behind me was the man carrying the text I had inquired about. His Holiness asked my monk friend, "What is that text?"

He replied, "That is the Lam Rim."

"Oh, be very careful with it," instructed His Holiness.

Once we were back outside, my monk friend and I were happily dancing around by the gate. "Now we have even received the blessings of speech from His Holiness the Dalai Lama," said my friend. "Not only that, I was also able to talk to him myself!" Even though the exchange was brief and impersonal, we both felt the importance and flow of grace from this meeting.

Some time later the monk said to me, "I am going to a monastery in Dalhousie to join some other monks. You are young. You could join the Tibetan Medical Institute there, but you would have to ask Dr. Yeshe Dhonden's permission to join."

When I went to ask the doctor, he first inquired whether I could read and write. When I said that I could, he had a student bring a block-lettered text. I read it. Then he had a cursive-scripted text brought. I read that also. "You read very well, but you will have to wait one week," he said. So I waited, but after a week our food was about to run out.

I returned to the house of Dr. Yeshe. "Still we have some organizing to do," he said. "You must wait another week."

My monk friend said, "He is probably old-fashioned and is expecting offerings. You don't have anything to offer, so you will have to keep waiting." Because I had no food left, I decided I had to get my things ready to go. Dividing what I had with my friend, I headed for Tso Pema, the most sacred of all waters for Tibetans.

The Lotus Lake

At the bus station, a Tibetan boy from Nepal helped me get on the right bus to Tso Pema, scribbling the words for Tso Pema in Hindi, so that I would know when to get down when the bus conductor shouted its name. Many people crowded into the bus, including some of my countrymen. It was nighttime when we reached the sacred lake. There I saw that people were circumambulating the lake continually, reciting mantras and making prayers of aspiration.

Some Tibetans had also opened bamboo shack restaurants, but because I had little money and no cooking pots, I just stayed under a tree without food. After some time I met Mr. Samdrup and his family, whom I knew from Tingri. When they found out I didn't have any means for cooking or a place to stay, they offered me food and accommodation. For two days I was treated very well. Later I met my acquaintance Khenpo Khensur from Lama Gyupa. We circumambulated and stayed together. I performed Chöd for him, which he very much enjoyed, and we became good friends.

The lake contained a number of little floating "islands" made of various branches and earth, with vegetation and small trees growing from them. These circulated constantly because of the huge lake's underwater currents; the islands were considered sacred parts of this holy site. Each tree in the lake even had its own name. However, the most prominent island had not been moving for some time. The Khenpo said, "If we do some purification, the tree island will circulate again." The next day was the tenth of the month, the day the monks and lamas did pujas, masked dances, and fire pujas. Khenpo gave me some incense to burn and a vase of water, and with these I went to the tree and offered prayers. The very moment we finished our puja, a flock of blackbirds flew up into the sky, noises emanated from the tree – and it started moving.

Everyone shouted, "Guru Rinpoche has arrived!" When the tree paused for a little bit on its journey, people hung prayer flags and katas. After thirty minutes, the tree finished a complete circle of the lake, and the smaller trees all followed. They were like boats moving by themselves, circumambulating the lake. The villagers said it had been a year since they had moved in that way.

Khenpo Khensur asked me to perform Chöd every evening. One evening he remarked, "You do Chöd very well. We live in Sikkim, where anyone who knows how to perform Chöd is considered very special. If you come with us, you will have a good life." I really felt like going with them, but somehow I had mixed feelings.

Continuing our pilgrimage, the Khenpo and his entourage of seven monks and I piled on board a bus bound for Amritsar in the Punjab. Once there, we entered the holy temple of the Sikhs. The walls were decorated with so many mirrors that you could see the reflections repeated ten times. The Punjabi Sikhs gave us as much dhal and bread as we could eat for free, but meat couldn't be eaten inside the temple. The Khenpo said this was Guru Rinpoche's blessing and we should eat here at least once. We stayed for two or three days.

We next went to Benares, staying and reading texts for several days at the request of a monk there. Finally we reached Bodhgaya, where many Tibetans, laypeople and monks, were circumambulating. Seeing the stupa built around the site where Shakyamuni Buddha attained enlightenment, I experienced a deep sense of faith. We lived in a courtyard for several days, performing our devotions. After a few days Khenpo was ready to return to Sikkim, and I was supposed to leave with him. Unclear about what I should do, I prostrated one hundred times in front of Buddha's statue and did Chöd practice. I asked the Buddha to grant me a dream that would tell me whether I should take the road to Sikkim or travel back to Nepal.

That night, I did have a dream. I was back in Nepal, in Boudha, circumambulating the stupa with two Tibetans. I couldn't remember how I had gotten there, and thought that this must be a dream. With disbelief I looked at the stupa. I saw the eyes of the stupa and all the prayer flags so clearly, I was certain it was real. I looked at the ground and noticed all the white and black stones and broken pebbles in great detail. Everything was completely lucid. In real life, outside the gate of the Boudha stupa, there was a chang shop called Khola Chenpo. The woman who worked there, Phurbu-la, was never angry or rude. A big brass bowl of chang, or barley beer, cost only twenty-five cents. It was delicious. Not only did it quench your thirst and fill your stomach, but you also became intoxicated! Because I had been in India for so long, drinking hot water, I wanted to drink some of this cold barley beer. By now I was convinced in my dream that I really must be in Boudha. I thought, "I need to go to Phurbu-la's place to have a drink." So I went to the dream chang shop. Usually it is very crowded inside, but this time there were very few people. In the middle of the shop was Phurbu-la, wearing a black sari and a white shawl and holding a big brass bowl of chang.

As soon as I entered, she said, "So you've come back, lama."

"Yes, I was in India and really missed your beer. All I could drink was boiled hot water. Now I'd really like a cup of chang."

She offered me the bowl and I grabbed it and drank the whole thing down in one long draught. The chang was cold and delicious, and I felt deeply happy. When I had finished, I looked up at her face. Right then I woke up and found myself still in Bodhgaya. I had a strong feeling of sadness and longing for my dream Boudha. I then realized that the Buddha had indeed given me a prophecy. It was clear in my heart that I should go to Kathmandu and not to the unfamiliar land of Sikkim. I told my friends about this, but they didn't really believe in my experience.

"You did not have a dream or prophecy; someone must have persuaded you to go to Nepal. Just forget about that." They insisted I go to Sikkim, but I also insisted that I did indeed have this dream, and that it was meaningful.

The Journey Home

The very next day I started my journey from Bodhgaya back to Nepal. As luck would have it, I met the very same Tibetan who had helped me find the bus to Tso Pema. He took me to the bus station and put me on the correct bus, saying, "Don't get off until they say 'Patna'. There you need to cross the river on a ferry." This was good information, because the whole time on the bus I was the only Tibetan and no one else spoke my language! In the evening, when the bus unloaded at Patna, all the people hurried to the river to try to get tickets. I also joined the rush, bought a ticket, and got on the boat.

This time the boat was quite large, and I wasn't afraid of its capsizing like before. Still, I was the only Tibetan in sight, even though there were quite a lot of people. Sitting quietly, I noticed that people were going up and down a flight of stairs on the boat. Because there was no one prohibiting people from using the stairs, I also climbed up to have a look. To my surprise there was a restaurant there, filled with people eating bread and potatoes!

I noticed two Nepalese people, who asked me in the Nepali language, "Where are you going?" When I said Kathmandu, they answered, "Sit with us." They bought me three small breads, potatoes, and sauce. Because I didn't have a guide, I asked whether we could travel together. "We aren't going back to Nepal right away," they answered. "We have some business to do. But if you are heading back, we can show you the way." When we finally got off the boat it was ten at night. Walking over some sand, we came to the station. My Nepalese friend pointed to an empty train and said, "This will take you to Nepal. Don't get out of this train until the conductor yells 'Raksol'!"

It was late and the doors of the train were locked, so they pushed me in through a window. Inside, I immediately fell into a deep sleep on the floor. When I awoke, the train was shaking and filled with people, a number of them standing right over me. When the conductor shouted "Raksol" I got off and bought some tea. Then I set out, crossing a small river, and headed toward some thatched houses. I knew I was close to home, because everyone spoke Nepalese. As I approached the village, someone cried, "Lama, Lama!" from one of the houses. It was a Sherpa family from Marme village by the Tibetan border, where I had lodged before. Finally, I met someone I knew! They offered me rice, dhal, meat, and chang. When I told them I was going back to Nepal, they gave me twenty rupees and put me on a small train traveling to the border.

When I got off the train, I found myself at the same place where I had originally arrived in India, where everyone had drunk tea from their unwashed pots. I slept alone under the very same tree that had sheltered me before. It might have been three or four in the morning when a Nepali boy shook me and called, "Hey lama, hey lama." I woke up and he asked, "Are you going to Kathmandu?"

"Yes, I am."

"Then come with me."

He took me to a truck that was ready to depart. A Sikh Punjabi man asked if I had eleven rupees, and when I said yes, he told me to get in. The boy said, "Climb up from behind." When I got on, I saw that the truck was full of goods, but there was some space in between the bags. "You stay here," the boy instructed. It was really quite comfortable and soft. I fell asleep while the truck rolled along, waking up only after we had stopped at a high mountain pass. I found the driver and the boy drinking tea in a shop.

They invited me to come down and join them, but I said, "I have a headache; I won't drink tea."

"Take your shawl off," the Punjabi man said. I took off my red silk outer robe and he tied it on my head. Then he massaged my hand very strongly. "Now go back up to the truck and sleep."

They stopped again just outside Kathmandu and insisted I come with them to eat. The driver gave me dhal, rice, and meat. Only in the morning light did I find out why the cargo was so comfortable – it was actually cotton! Finally we arrived in the city, and the driver asked for his eleven rupees. I gave him the money and felt happy knowing exactly where I was and that I was once again able to find my way around by myself after so many strange lands. But as I started to walk away, the driver came running after me. At first I was scared, thinking that I hadn't paid properly, but it turned out I had simply left my lama's shawl on the truck.

In a restaurant nearby, I saw my friend Ngawang Dorje eating yogurt and beaten rice. He invited me to join him and bought me some food. After that I started to walk from the city towards Boudha, several miles away. Along the way a jeep stopped for me, and it happened to be my friend Tseten Namgyal driving, so I had a ride all the way to Boudha. By the time I arrived it was evening, and people were already circumambulating the stupa. Surrounded by friends, I was in the Boudha of my dreams – now a reality again.

Teachings on Death and Other Stories

In the Sherpa village once again, I stayed at the house of Ibi Karma for three years. Ibi Kamra was 88 years old then, and she lived to be 100. Now, her grandson often visits my monastery.

Since I had left my wife in Tibet, I had lived alone, and I also drank my fair share of rakshi, or Nepalese wine. The people thought I was a fully ordained monk and called me the village Gelong. Whatever they grew – corn, vegetables, or potatoes – they would kindly offer their first crop to me. By then, so many new Tibetans had arrived in the village that each Sherpa house had two Tibetan families living in it. There were also many people from the Nyalam region.

Some Tibetans would stay one year, and then go off to Kathmandu, or to Tanto Pani, which was closer by. Others settled in different Sherpa villages, some in Jawalekhel, and some in India. Many people suggested I should also go to India. But I told them, "I've already been and I'm not going again."

But because of the crowded conditions, unclean water, and unfamiliar heat, many people were dying, especially the children and the elderly. I was kept very busy performing all the Powa, Chöd practices, and funeral rituals. Sometimes I had to dispose of the bodies in the river, where I was often bitten by leeches. At times I had to cut up the bodies before I threw them into the water. The fishermen were catching a lot of human flesh in their nets, and the fish probably didn't like it very much either! Each day I did this kind of work for the dead, traveling everywhere in the area. Many people advised me, "If you work like this every day and night, you yourself will get sick." But I never became ill, and I continued with these practices.

One day, a monk named Urgyen Kelsong asked me to come to their thatched house to perform Chöd for his father, who had died in Tanto Pani. As I was performing the ritual, a sound was emitted from the dead father's mouth. All the people in the room ran out the door in terror, thinking a demon or a god had caused this. In Tibet, there is always the fear that the corpse will wake up and become a zombie. Getting up, I saw that the body was swollen around the neck. I hit his neck area twice with my thighbone trumpet. Urine immediately poured out of him, and some strange vapors came out of his mouth. The next morning I had to place his body in the Tanto Pani River.

Nearby was another Tibetan family named Sharpie, from northern Tibet. The husband was a strong man, but he died quite suddenly, and they asked me to do the funeral. There were three or four brothers who were helping the widow, and the younger brother – who walked with a limp – was a very good text reader. At night I asked him to help me read the prayers. He sat in one corner of the room, while I stayed in the other corner with the rest of the brothers. I felt a little drowsy and dozed off for a bit, and when I awoke all the brothers were running out of the room, one after the other. I had no idea what was going on, but just picked up my damaru and continued the practice. The young brother had also stopped beating the drum.

"What's going on?" I asked him.

"He's saying something!" he blurted out.

"Who is?" I asked. With a shaking finger, the boy pointed toward the corpse. I put my drum down to listen. Indeed, from the corpse I heard the sound, "Garrard!"

At first I was also scared, and then I became angry. As I removed the cotton cloth that covered the corpse to see what was happening, my helper ran away. The dead body was swollen and its hair was standing on end, as if it were coming back to life. Blowing the kangling did not help, but the grandfather cleverly brought me some sand.

I visualized and then spoke a mantra into the sand and threw it on the corpse. The dead body immediately threw up blood and urinated, such that the room was soiled with these fluids, and the sounds ceased. The other brothers were still nowhere to be found, so I hired two people and we wrapped the body in a white blanket. Carrying him to the riverside, I did Chöd practice. When I opened the blanket, vapors came out of the body, and we then disposed of it in the river. Overall I did about forty funeral services in that area, but these were the only times that this kind of manifestation happened. No other bodies emitted sounds or had any unusual occurrences.

The village people continually came to me for help. When someone became sick, I gave them a mantra to recite and some medicines. They would pass frogs and lizards in their feces, and then recover. If poor people died, I took my own supplies to the family to perform the funeral rites. To those Tibetans who had no food, I would give a large bag of corn. If a husband died leaving his wife and children alone, I would try to find the widow a house and some kind of a job. But in those days, if you had ten rupees you were rich!

After the exodus from Tibet had died down, I spent three years in closed retreat near Singatrak Rinpoche's Monastery, just above Tatopani Village.

Settling in Kathmandu

I returned to Kathmandu where the Tibetans were all occupied making carpets, spinning wool or sewing clothes. I was invited to do many pujas and was soon quite busy. I stayed in the Jawalekhel refuge camp, doing rituals at people's homes, whether it was a rented apartment or a thatched cottage. It was during this time I met my present wife. After some time, the Sherpas came to find me and bring me back to their village. "I've already agreed to stay here one year and help the Tibetans in Jawalekhel," I said. "You may use whatever things I still have there in the village." I gave them some gifts and sent them back home. Indeed, since that time I have not been able to return to the village.

There were a number of Swiss people helping the Tibetans in the camp, and they generally treated me very well. One particular Swiss Red Cross worker named Mrs. Fisherson told me, "If you only practice Dharma, you might have enough money for food, but if you have enough money for only food, you won't have enough for clothes. Instead of only Dharma, why don't you work?"

"I don't know any work; what should I do?" I asked.

She said she would teach me an easy technique, and proceeded to show me how to graph carpet designs on paper. I learned this very quickly, and later found out that I was the first person in Nepal to ever design carpets using this method, because traditionally we never used graphs. My method was simple: I would recite Padampa Sangye's mantra before going to sleep, and I would have a dream for a graph design. When I awoke, I drew what I saw in my dream. This worked very well! My salary at that time was three rupees a day. And every day, Mrs. Fisherson would bring me two chocolates – I had never had these before!

The camp in Jawalekhel was directed by a Tibetan man who was a Gelugpa monk. He seemed to dislike me, and did not treat me very well. This director had one Tibetan maid. She and her husband had once been nomads, and now her husband carved mantras on stones, which he would then sell.

The director appointed me to teach the husband how to graph carpet designs. At that time, I was the only person able to graph big designs from small pictures, which was very difficult work. I worked there for six years until the Swiss woman was transferred. She threw a party for me, at which she told everyone that I was the only one who could design large carpets and that I should be paid very well. The Swiss people also repeated this to the Tibetan director – that I should be paid better. The Swiss woman said, "Though this man isn't learned in languages, he works very hard and is talented."

The Swiss director then was replaced by a Nepalese man. He saw the situation and said, "This lama has been paid very poorly. In Nepalese tradition, the designer is supposed to be paid more. This man has only enough to buy morning bread."

He thus increased my salary to five rupees a day. But the Tibetan director objected, saying, "This man is like Milarepa. He can survive on nettles. He doesn't need a raise." The Swiss woman, in my defense, again protested. "Milarepa was also a sentient being. This is unfair." After that, the Nepalese not only raised my salary, but also gave me an apartment to stay in. Thus I worked there for three more years.

Meanwhile, sick people with toothaches, mental problems, and every kind of ailment came to me for healing. Though other lamas had not been able to cure them, I was able to help. If their teeth hurt, I just did mantras for their teeth. If someone had had a stroke, I would do a puja and they would get well again. If there was a death in the camp, they would listen to only my advice. If a poor person died, I would carry the body and do the Chöd ritual myself.

These activities made these families happy and satisfied. If any people fell in love, they would come to me for a divination to see whether they should marry If I told them it was okay to marry, and they followed my advice, their marriage was successful. If the divination didn't come out well, I tell them not to marry. But sometimes they would ask for a special ritual, and decide to live together anyway. I have found that such marriages usually end up in divorce!

Later they nicknamed me Popo Lama – grandfather lama. If the children fell down or were hurt in the schoolyard, they would cry, "Get Popo Lama!" I would come and blow on the wound and their pain would quickly vanish.

Meeting My Son from Tibet

My wife and I had a daughter we named Tsomo, and shortly after her birth I heard news of my son back in Tibet. I really wanted to meet him. The news came from my son's wife's cousin, who had just moved to Nepal. I gave the cousin some money to bring my son back from Tibet.

After three months, my son arrived, accompanied by another boy his same age. They were waiting for me at the cousin's house when I got back from a puja. My wife had offered to pick him up, but the cousin insisted that I come personally. The cousin decided to tease me. "So you are so smart, can you tell me which of these two boys is your son?"

I looked at both boys, and I knew immediately which one was my son. "That one is my boy!" I shouted with a smile. Everyone laughed.

He stayed for two months and I sent them back with many gifts, clothes, food, and money. These days, my son often comes to visit me.

The Black Protection Cord

I recited Padampa Sangye's mantra on black protection cords; imparting blessings that would help students avoid any obstacles. Everyone wore these cords, and even when they were older and went away to college, I gave them each a cord. They felt protected and happy. Wherever they went, to Dharamsala or Mussoorie, they would always receive this sacred kind of amulet. If the children traveled on a plane or a bus, they would ask each other if they had Popo Lama's protection cords. Several told me that even if they were having trouble sleeping, by wearing this cord at night they could have a restful night.

However, one teacher in Dharamsala repeatedly cautioned a student about this. "You shouldn't wear a black cord," he said. "It may be bad, as this is from the Chinese tradition." Whenever the student, whose name was Thundrup, wore the black protection cord, the teacher would scold him. The boy thought to himself, "I'm not allowed to wear this, but if I don't, I don't sleep well, and I will have other obstacles." So the young boy went into the bathroom, cut the cord into small pieces and swallowed it!

He thought that in this way he would have the cord close to his heart. When Thundrup sent this story to his father in a letter, the father asked for my advice. I told him, "This teacher may have a lot of knowledge, but he doesn't know the dharma. According to Buddhist tradition, a protection cord may be red, yellow, blue or black. If he ate this cord, it will still benefit him and he will feel protected. There is no problem."

After some time, several young girls fainted at the Songtsen School in Boudha, one after the other, and other strange things started happening there. The school had many pujas performed to remove these obstacles, but it didn't help. More students were passing out every day. Finally, they invited me to come there to try to solve the problem.

The morning I arrived, the principal asked me to give a lecture on education. All the students of various ages, along with all the teachers, gathered in the yard. I took the opportunity to give a lecture on the black protection cords.

The Buddha taught 84,000 teachings, each according to one's own capacity, sometimes gentle and sometimes wrathful. For every illness there is a cure, but when karma runs out, death comes. You are students and don't have much time for this right now, so don't worry about all the different deities in Buddhism.

But at least you should know about the four directions: east, west, south, north – and center. The sun rises in the east, to our front. To our right is considered south, the back is west, and the left is north. The five colors apply to these directions: East is white, south is yellow, west is red, north is green – and the center is dark blue. Our whole physical being arises from these five elements of the five colors. The white Water in the east is expressed as the fluids and blood of all sentient beings. The yellow Earth in the south comprises the flesh and bones of beings. The red Fire in the west gives beings energy and warmth. The green Wind in the north is how we derive breath and motion. And from the blue Space in the center comes mind, consciousness.

Sentient beings come from these five elements – and at death they all separate. When these five directions are seen in the form of deities, east is white Vajrasattva, south is yellow Ratnasambhava, west is red Amitabha, north is green Amoghasiddhi, and finally – space is blue Vairocana. Each is in embrace with its consort, so they are the duality of male and female. If you practice with the yellow deity, you get the blessing of the earth element, and so on. This is how the deities function, and that is why there are different colored protection cords.

One can also see our being as divided into three. The body or form is allocated the white color and the letter Om, situated at our forehead. The power of speech is considered to be a red Ah at our throat. And the quality of mind is seen as a blue Hung in the heart area. Each represents a different deity – Manjushri, Chenrezig, and

Vajrapani. All three are condensed into Padampa Sangye. His color is very dark and rich. Dampa's deity is the black Vajrayogini or Troma Nagmo. For that reason the mantra is also black.

Thus the black cord is actually a deep dark blue, and it represents the Buddha's mind. It has nine sacred knots in a row, and it protects from nine harmful things: weapons, wild animals and other physical harm, formless beings such as demons and ghosts, and so forth.

There are different kinds of ghosts. The Tsen are red, Dü are black demons, Lha or god-like entities are white, Za or astrological demons are multicolored, Nyen is yellow, and Nagas – demons of water and earth – are green. The mind of all the Buddhas must be evoked to expel the harm caused by these formless beings. This invocation happens through the black color and the deity Vajrapani, and through the black syllable Hum. When the nine sacred knots are tied, the mantra Hum is chanted to impart this powerful purifying effect to the protection cord.

So it is directly from the Buddha's teachings that I made these black cords, and not from any Chinese tradition. It may have been just ignorance about Dharma, or perhaps jealousy, but some people have the mistaken idea that protection cords are only red, and that black cords must be from the Chinese. The truth is, I have met only two Chinese people in my whole life – – and that was in Nepal, not Tibet!

I explained all this to the teachers and students at the Songtsen School. I then did a Chöd practice and chased away the negative entities, using a dough effigy or "ransom torma". Then I taught the students how to recite all the appropriate mantras. After that, all the sicknesses and strange occurrences at the school ceased.

Possession

Padampa Sangye's mantra has been very useful in helping people. One time, the mother of a particular secretary became possessed by a demon. She had visited many hospitals and healers, but they were unable to help her. They brought her to me, but when I tried to do some ritual healing, she started shouting wildly.

I asked her, "Who is speaking?"

The demon said, "I am a man-eating devil. I eat people, and now I will eat you, lama."

"If you will eat me, then eat me now," I replied. "Take my flesh; take my bones. Eat me now."

The woman behaved as if she were trying to consume me, but she gradually became tired and slowed down her agitation. Visualizing Dampa Sangye and Machig Labdron, I uttered a sudden, loud "PHAT!" and with that she fell down unconscious. I sprinkled water on her and she slowly woke up.

"I'm sorry. I'm sorry, lama," she said.

I asked the demon, "Why did you do this to her?"

The demon's voice replied, "I was harming her because she did a lot of business but did not help me."

"Do not harm her any more. You have already accumulated many non-virtuous actions," I admonished this devil. Then I further assured it, "People will help you from now on. Just drink some water." The demon drank the water and immediately left the body of the woman. Over time, she became completely well again.

The Last 100,000

For a while then, I spent my time doing just pujas, such that I was working day and night for different families. But I was also drinking a lot, sometimes as much as twelve glasses at a time. After about four years of overworking and drinking, I gradually became sick. I went to doctors, and I took their medicines, but it did not help. Many doubts arose and I thought, "I have not even killed an insect in my life. Why am I sick?"

Suddenly I remembered my lama's words in Tibet. "If you do the preliminaries three times, visit funeral sites and go on pilgrimage for one year, this will be enough. You won't need to receive instructions from any other lamas." I had done 100,000 prostrations at my lama's monastery and 100,000 at Machig's cave, but I had not completed the third set of 100,000. Perhaps I was now ill because I had not finished all that my lama had intended for me?

I found a place to live in front of the Swayambhu stupa, and I began to offer my 100,000 prostrations. It was an old Nepalese style house, and living just above me on the third floor were some Tibetan nomad families. I lived on the middle floor, and on the ground floor were stored supplies. I thought that obstacles might come about from living in this house, because it was so old.

One time I had a visit from three renowned lamas, Urgyen Tulku, Saptru Rinpoche, and Dapsang Rinpoche.

Urgyen Tulku spoke to me. "If you want to offer prostrations here, many people might come and bother you. I can give you a room at my monastery where you will have solitude." But I told him that I had already begun, and it was too late to move. However, in order to prevent any obstacles or disturbances to my prostrations, I did a Chöd practice each evening.

One night after Chöd practice, I fell into a deep sleep, and I had an unusual dream. The door was closed when I went to bed, but in this dream I woke up and found the door open – and the light was on. An old Nepalese woman stood there, with white-combed hair and a full set of teeth, wearing a green gown and a white shawl. She didn't move, but just looked at me intently. I wondered why she had come here in the middle of the night. "What do you want?" I asked.

And she immediately vanished. I got up and came out of my room to see if she had gone to the third floor to visit the nomads, but I saw that all of them were sleeping. Then I went to check to find out whether the main gate was opened. When I saw that it was still closed and locked, I thought that the appearance of the woman must have been a supernatural sign from the demons. Thinking this, I returned to my room and went back to sleep. But again the same woman appeared. This time, though, her body had a monkey's head and it was screeching. I thought this must certainly be a sign. I shouted, "PHEY!" and she vanished.

The next morning an old man from Jawalakhel came for a divination for his family. I put my dice on the table and offered the man some tea. Meanwhile, a monkey appeared at the windowsill, and it snatched my dice! I had a very strange feeling about the woman last night and the monkey today. The demon was able to take my dice, but no other obstacle arose. So I just continued on with my prostrations.

The Gelug Lama Visits

One day, while I was sweating very profusely from my prostrations, I had a visit from a man wearing robes and a cloth on his head to keep off the heat. When he sat down on the floor, I recognized him as high Gelug lama, Sekung Rinpoche. I immediately offered him cushions to sit on, but he refused. "Oh I don't need those," he said. "I don't mind sitting on the floor. You use them, as you must be tired from all your prostrations."

After a while, some children came by. The lama gave them five rupees to go buy some candy. When they returned, he put all the candy on the floor. "Now I have made tsok," he said, "and there are five left over for you." The kindly lama then gave me five pieces of candy, and he gave the rest to the children.

The lama then stood up and asked me what prayers I had been saying. After I told him, he said, "This is good, but it would be better if you said, 'OM NAMO MANJUSHRIYE NAMO SUSHRIYE NAMO UTTAMA SHRIYE SOHA' as your prayer. This will multiply the merit of your prostrations many times." I agreed to recite that. Sekung Rinpoche then asked me to lend him my prayer beads. He took them to the stupa, and holding my beads in his folded hands, he spoke many prayers with them. Then he gave them back to me and advised, "Just relax, do your prostrations well, and enjoy."

In spite of the lama's kindness and attentiveness, his appearance was unstable; he seemed to me as if drunk. I decided to visit Rinpoche at his own monastery, which was situated just below Swayambhu stupa. I found rice and tea in his room there as if he was preparing to do a puja, and a picture of His Holiness the Dalai Lama hung on the wall. Rinpoche moved over on his seat when I entered, and he asked me to sit next to him. "We are on the same level," he said.

Out of politeness and respect for his position, though, I did not accept his offer and instead sat on the bed opposite him. "I like it here better," I said.

"Have you come on a pilgrimage?" he asked.

"Yes," I replied. "I haven't seen His Holiness and his teachers for a while. Where are they these days?" At that point I realized that his mind and memory were no longer clear. "Oh, His Holiness is living in Dharamsala and doing well. He said that he hopes you are staying well, and he wishes you health."

He then prostrated three times. "Thank you very much," he said. "Thank you very much. I practice Palden Lhamo, Gadon, and Nechung but they never appeared to me. But for you they all appeared, and they look after you. Please do a puja for me."

His attendant then asked me, "Where do you stay?"

"I live in Jawalakhel," I replied.

"This morning Rinpoche announced that many people were coming to put up prayer flags – though nothing like this is happening today – and he had us bring down the pictures from the assembly hall. He has been causing so many problems lately. Please do a puja for us."

Thus learning about the Rinpoche's condition, I did a puja in his room. Rinpoche became very happy and thanked us. He asked his attendant to bring the largest kata (a ceremonial scarf) that he could find. It was so long that I had to fold it several times around my neck.

Then he took five rupees from his white wallet and said, "Drink chang with this. Don't worry, if you get too drunk you can stay here." It seemed to me as though Rinpoche's condition had given him clairvoyance – how did he know I liked to drink chang?

Then he asked me, "Do you perform Chöd?"

When I replied, "Yes I do," he said, "Machig Labdron was a great practitioner. Please practice well yourself." Again it seemed to me that the Rinpoche had some deeper insight, in spite of his problems. The attendants then asked me to leave, but as I was departing, the Rinpoche ran after me with a blanket, saying, "I'm coming with you."

In order to calm him, they had to tell him, "This lama is going to Swayambu on pilgrimage, but he will be back later. You can meet him in the evening." After this incident, I encountered no more obstacles or distractions, and I was able to finish all my prostrations. I offered some butter lamps in thanks and returned to Jawalakhel.

Chang Stories

I was now 30 years old, and I was eating and drinking too much. I had gradually become quite fat, so I tried to minimize my drinking. Once day I ran into some old Khampa friends and got very drunk with them in a local chang shop. I had 18 cups of chang and four cups of liquor. The barmaid cut me off, because she didn't think I'd be able to get home safely. She asked my Kampa friends to look after me. I don't remember what happened after that, but the following story was told to me later by several amused friends.

On our way home, a black bull and a brown bull were fighting near an army camp in Patan, and this had gathered a large crowd of onlookers. Ditching my Khampa friends, I went straight to the place where the bulls were fighting. The Nepalese people said, "The bulls will kill lama!" But I didn't hear them. I just pulled up my robes and "mooned" both of the bulls, showing them my naked bottom. The bulls suddenly stopped fighting, looking curiously at my behind.

Then, in Hindi, I told the black bull to leave. He walked away. I then asked the brown bull to sit down. The bull sat down, and I climbed onto his back and talked to him in some unknown Indian language. The bull then got up and walked me slowly toward my home. After a ways, the bull sat down again and I slid off him and staggered under a tree to go to sleep. I had only my mala beads in my hands and was wearing only my lower robe. Somehow, I didn't have my shirt any more. Apparently, someone took a photo of me on the bull, and another photo of me passed out under a tree.

I left my Mala beads under that tree, and later an old man found them. Thinking he might be able to sell them to some tourists, he put them in the window of his shop. But that night my beads transformed themselves into a black snake. The old man was so terrified of the snake that he was not able to sleep. The next morning, however, my rosary was just made of beads again. Still shaken, the old man went to the camp and asked whose beads those were. Naturally, everyone recognized them, and someone brought them back to me.

A few days later, though, the police came with the photos, and asked whether I knew this person. I had no memory of the events of that night, so I said I didn't recognize him.

They told me how I had ridden the bull and then passed out under a tree. But the photo was really amazing – it shows me in a very powerful position with my arm raised above my head, my eyes blazing – and I had a slight mustache. People made copies of this photo and told me later that it helped them heal headaches when they kept it near the head of their bed at night.

Once there was a girl who was mentally ill. When she would come to visit me, she would behave normally and feel fine. But when she got home, she would be crazy again. She even stayed for a week with me and was getting better – but when she went home again, she became mentally ill again. So I gave them this photo, which they still have in their house, and the girl has been fine.

Another time, I took my bell to a blacksmith to have it repaired. While it was there with the blacksmith, I decided to sit down in a chang shop next door. It was a hot day, and trying to refresh myself, I drank too much and became drunk. Later, as I walked back home, I dropped my bell somewhere along the way. A Nepalese man found it and took it home with him, and the bell rang by itself all night long. The next morning he decided he had better take it outside; he rang the bell loudly to see if he could find its owner. I was retracing my route of the previous day, looking for the bell, and I saw the man not far from the chang shop, ringing my bell frantically. "That's my bell," I said. He replied, "Please, just take it! I found it on the road and took it home, but the bell just rang by itself all night. Please take it back!"

Someone once offered me 30,000 rupees to do a puja. My Chöd friends and I went to Namo Buddha to perform the ritual; I circumambulated the stupa and went to a shop to drink some rakshi. There were more than 20 Tibetan pilgrims from the border area there, and I gave these Tibetans 1,000 rupees each. When my friends asked me where the money was in order to do the shopping for the puja, I told them I had given it all away. "It is all gone."

My friends argued with me. "You gave all the money away, now we don't have enough money to take the bus home, let alone do a puja!" "In this place the Buddha gave his flesh and bones to a tigress," I replied. "There is nothing wrong if I give mere paper alms to these people. You should try giving your body to a tigress!"

One friend said, "But now it is time to make noodle soup and there is no meat to add."

I said, "Why don't you just put that dog in the soup."

That night all my friends were angry with me. They put together 100 rupees and bought enough for a small tsok.

Meanwhile, a rich Sherpa from Bhaktapur and his religious wife had come to Namo Buddha. The wife offered us 60,000 rupees! Look what happens when you give alms. We had 30,000 rupees and I gave it all away, and then we got 60,000 in return. It's a good lesson in giving.

All of my friends were changed after this. They became less stingy and more open, and they really began to believe in me.

Other Lamas

In Jawalakhel I lived next to two rich old Tibetans. One man lived alone, and the other had two sons. The one who was from Dzong Gha was already rich when he lived in Tibet. Previously, he had gone to Lhasa to offer long life pujas to His Holiness the Dalai Lama, and he had also sponsored many pujas in Nepal. Over the years, each of these men had me read texts in his home, and whenever I went on pilgrimage I always liked to take these two old gentlemen with me.

At one time, Dudjom Rinpoche came to consecrate the new awning on the Boudhanath stupa after it had been hit by lightning. While he was staying in Kathmandu, many other Rinpoches and lay people also came to visit. One of the two old men wanted to meet Dudjom Rinpoche, and he asked me to help arrange this. So one morning we went to Boudha and obtained an audience with Rinpoche. The old man offered dzi stones, mani stones, silver coins, texts written in gold and many other precious things. Rinpoche asked me, "Are you the son of this old man?"

"I'm not his son, Rinpoche. I am a practitioner and he is my patron and neighbor. I perform pujas in his home and I also take him with me when I go on pilgrimage."

"This is very good," he said. "Meditators should be like that. All men are your father, all women are your mother, and all children are your children. You should practice like this until you die. You should consider this man your father and he should consider you his son."

I had also brought all the texts in the Long Chen Nying Thig. "I have received some transmissions from my lama in Tibet," I told Rinpoche. "But there are many Tibetans for whom I have to do a lot of pujas. Sometimes I have to do 'Offering to the deities' but I don't have this transmission. Can you give this to me?"

Rinpoche said, "I don't have the book right now."

"I brought it with me."

"In that case I can give you the transmission. If I don't give transmission to practitioners, who else am I supposed to give them to?" Then Rinpoche gave me all the transmissions. He also gave ritual medallions with mantras in them to me and the two old men. "By just wearing these, you will be free from non-virtuous acts," he said. We all felt very happy.

The next time we met Dudjom Rinpoche, he came to Thamel. We did tsok puja and sang Chöd songs for him. At the time, the man who had offered so many things to Rinpoche was very worried about losing his eyesight. Rinpoche advised him, "Just as soon as you get up, before drinking anything, you should recite the mani mantra twenty times for at least one session every morning. Then blow out the mantra onto your ring finger and massage your eyes. If you do this, I guarantee you will never lose your eyesight." The old man followed the instructions carefully and never did lose his sight.

When the old man died, Dudjom Rinpoche did the Powa service and we were able to offer him the old man's belongings. This old man had once given me a stone that had the images of the sun and moon on it. This stone is now inside the statue of Padampa Sangye in my monastery.

I met many special lamas while living in Nepal and visiting India. Out of gratitude, I believe it is important to mention them by name. In Nepal, my lamas were Dudjom Rinpoche, Chatral Rinpoche, Dodrupchen Rinpoche, Penor Rinpoche, Ugyen Tulku, Tratuk Rinpoche, Sekung Rinpoche, Sapchu Rinpoche, Lungbum Rinpoche, Tsatrul Rinpoche, Dilgo Kyentse, Moktsa Rinpoche, and Singetrak Rinpoche.

In India my lamas were His Holiness the Dalai Lama, Yongsen Ling Rinpoche, Tema Lojur Rinpoche, Tsenshap Rinpoche, Minling

Trichen, Trakyewae'i lama, Gelong Gyalpo, Koyak Geshe, and Lolo Geshe.

A Visit to a Long-Life Cave

Shortly after my friend's death, I made a visit to Guru Rinpoche's Long Life Cave, called Maratika, with 10 Tibetans, 25 Nepalis from Manang, and 10 Sherpas from Solukumbu. I performed a long life puja for them, an offering ceremony for Guru Rinpoche. The Manangis and Sherpas offered lots of things to Guru Rinpoche, including many large containers of Chang. I gave blessing items for healing to the people and drank some chang too. The Manangis and Sherpas drank almost two large containers each. We were all pretty drunk.

That night, I went to a tall cliff for a walk, and everyone thought I had fallen down the cliff. Later, someone found me sleeping in my bed and everyone had a laugh about it.

The son of the lama who lives in the area had too much to drink and couldn't walk. So we put him on a red horse to go back to Kathmandu, while we all piled back onto the airplane.

Upon hearing about our good time at the cave, a man named Sesok Kelsang from Dharamsala wanted to sponsor another puja by me. He came to visit and told me he'd like a puja in Rikeswor, India, and 140 people from my Sangha came to participate. After we offered the puja and hung prayer flags, we went down to the river where there is a rock that naturally looks like Guru Rinpoche. We did a smoke offering. From the rock came water, and then came a white fluid, just like milk. It was a real blessing.

Meeting Sangye Paljor

That year Chatral Rinpoche asked me to come and receive the teachings from Dodrupchen Rinpoche, who was visiting there. There were about 100 other people also receiving the teachings. He gave the transmissions, empowerments, and explanations for the entire Long Chen Nying Thig. Dodrupchen now resides in Sikkim.

One year after that, Chatral Rinpoche brought Motsa Rinpoche from Tibet. He was a lama of Kathok Dorjeden monastery in Tibet. In Kathok monastery, there were two high lamas, Rinchen Longsar and Dudul Dorje. The two lamas had written 20 volumes of texts. It was from these 20 texts that Motsa Rinpoche taught.

The teachings were given in Godavari. We all had to pitch tents. My tent was a Khampa style tent, made by Khampas. One day there was a strong wind and all the tents were blown away, except for my tent. All the other practitioners were left without tents.

There was a westerner named Sangye Paljor who was also receiving teachings. He was very surprised that all the tents were blown away except one. With curiosity, he investigated inside and outside my tent, and then came to meet me.

"Maybe it wasn't blown away because of the protection cord I hung on the tent wall," I suggested to him.

"It must be true," he said, "because the ropes and tent pegs were stronger on the other tents. Yours should have easily blown away, but it did not. It must be the protection cord."

After that Sangye Paljor gained great faith in the protection cord. He took many back with him to London. He comes twice a year to

Nepal. Sometimes he asks for divinations from me. Once he checked my divination with that of other lamas and found my suggestions to be more effective. He speaks both Nepalese and Tibetan. We spoke deeply and became very good friends. He advised me to stop drinking so much – advice I took to heart – and these days I don't drink very much at all.

The People's Lama

After I had been away for a month, the Tibetans in the camp said I had been gone for far too long. I engaged myself in doing pujas and helping the families after that. While I helped Tibetans do pujas, funerals, and healings in Jawalakhel, I would also design carpets and draw graphs in the factory. One day the people in the camp got together for a meeting and said, "If the lama is graphing and designing he will not be able to do pujas for us at the same time. It is more important that he does this religious work for us."

The older people of the camp requested permission from the camp official that I be allowed to leave my job in order to help the refugee families. So I trained three young Tibetans to do the job and then left.

As I was leaving, though, the director asked for me to come see him. "The older people have suggested that you leave your job. Because you are no longer doing business and are just doing Dharma to benefit the people of the camp, I can't tell you not to leave. This is important. But when there are pujas for His Holiness, you should come to help out."

When the leaders of the camp invited other lamas to do pujas the children said, "Why is Popo Lama not here?" Again, I had to attend these other pujas as well. The camp director became worried and had another talk with me.

I explained to him, "If you ask me to come, I will come. There is no problem." So I always attended when asked.

The Refugee Camp

One day, the people who had eaten all my tsampa and butter when I was in India came to live in the refugee camp. They asked me to do a puja for them. I did the puja, but they acted very poorly afterwards. They became drunk and spoke rudely to me, "Get out of here."

I said, "It's okay, I'll leave."

Later they had many obstacles in their lives and asked me to come do a puja again.

Also in the camp was a man from my village in Tingri. Because we were from the same village, he was nice to me. I taught him how to graph carpets and he invited me to do pujas. Once he asked me to do a divination for his marriage. I suggested a good date for him to get married.

He did marry, and things went very well for him. He ran a small business and his wife wove carpets. When he went away on business, I would come to watch the kids and do pujas for the week. Later they became very rich, and then they asked me to leave. "Go away," they said.

I said, "It is not a problem."

Many high lamas and other rich people asked me to do pujas. However, they never asked me to leave or to not come back. They weren't rude to me like some others had been.

When I first started doing pujas in Jawalakhel, I would get five rupees a day. Back then I just ate bread and wheat porridge. After three or four years I was being paid ten rupees per day. These days, of course, they offer much more. If people are rich they may offer five hundred rupees, those who are not usually offer one hundred.

Though many families had houses, I lived in a single room given to me by the camp. Some rich patrons expressed the opinion that I should have a house. I didn't have the money, so I didn't consider building one.

The Fruition

In Patan there was a Newari couple; the man came from a low caste farmer's family and the wife came from a high caste family. They did not ask their parents for permission and married against social customs. The girl's family felt embarrassed and literally forced them out of town to live in an open field. They built a small house with one wooden pillar, slept on the bare ground, and had but a modest kitchen. The husband came to me one day and requested a puja. "Our parents have kicked us out," he explained. "We are very poor. Please do a puja of wealth for us."

Feeling great compassion for this young couple, with their shabby clothing and modest house, I went with another friend to do a puja for them. There was hardly any room in the house, and the wind blew straight through the wooden walls. I asked them to bring me a vase, into which I put all the holy objects and a blessing. But my friend refused to recite the text with me.

"Why are you not reciting the ritual?" I asked. "Are you sick?"

He angrily said, "They are so poor! Their wooden walls are so cold I felt sick and nauseated all day. We could have done a puja for a rich family today; why didn't we go there? You are crazy."

I looked at him sternly and said, "You are wrong! Dharma is for all people. If you do Dharma for the poor, it is more beneficial. If you do it for the benefit of the rich only, then it is like selling Dharma."

After a year, that same Newari man came to see me again. He asked me to do a wealth puja once more, and to help him with a problem. When I arrived at his home, there were three truckloads of logs and firewood piled up in the field in front of his house. "In the mountains, a woman's husband died. She owns a forest and a truck, and she has asked me to sell her wood for her. She will supply the wood and I will pay her later. Should I do this? Will I be able to carry it out?"

After I performed a divination, I told him, "Now the gods are taking care of you. You should be brave and carry on the business, but be careful to pay her on time. You will make a good profit and it will be very successful." He was satisfied with this and decided to follow my advice.

Meanwhile, the carpet industry was booming. All the carpet factories needed wood for their looms, and all the buyers came to this man for their supplies. In three years' time, he had sold so much wood that he had become quite rich. After that, he took care of me in many ways. He put up a wood panel in my home, to keep rats and vermin out. Later, a rat managed to eat a hole in the wood panel, and when the man visited me again, he saw the rat run right out of the hole in my wall. "I feel very sad that my lama is living with rats," he said. "Because I have a good wood business, whatever lumber you need to build a new house, I will give to you."

Meanwhile, a Kagyu lama consulted me regarding some trouble he was having at his monastery. Though he was a good scholar and had been educated in Varanasi, he had begun to doubt whether he should stay there or strike off on his own. I did the divination and said, "You are good in languages, and you are a handsome man. The other monks have become jealous of you. Now, do not stay in that monastery any longer, but go to a Nyingma lama to receive an empowerment. You should become a Nyingma practitioner and eventually go to the West to teach."

"If this will benefit me, then I will do it," he replied.

I did a wealth puja for him and gave him a protection cord. He left, and he traveled to Germany, Denmark, and Switzerland. Later he became extremely wealthy, and when he returned from the West, he built a large house in Boudha and then built his own monastery.

"Please come to my home," he asked me. "I will offer you a mandala." But instead of a traditional mandala, he offered me a huge plate piled with thousands of rupee notes. I had never in my life seen so much money.

I said, "I am a yogi; this money is not necessary for me."

"All right then," he replied. "But you shouldn't live like this. One man has already offered you wood. I will offer you bricks. Please build a house."

I told no one but my friend Tenzin Dorje about these offers. A carpet-seller, his wife had died of poisoning some years previously. Of course I had performed all her funeral pujas. He too had became quite well off, and he told me, "Because other people have offered you wood and bricks, I will give you all the iron and steel you need to build your house."

At this time there was a successful married Khampa woman who was very close to my heart. I had taken care of her when she was small, and I had helped her when she was sick. Hearing of these other acts of generosity, she offered to buy me all the cement for my house. I then told my wife's brother all about the wood, bricks, iron and cement, and I asked him, "Should I build a house or not?"

"Ah, you were probably drunk," he said. "You drink too much chang! There isn't anyone these days who will give things away like that."

"No," I said, "this is not a dream. There really are people offering me these things." Still he didn't believe me, so he got on his motorbike and visited all the families who had kindly offered these things. Afterward, he felt ashamed, as all the families were upset with him for his doubt and negative attitude.

The family of my wife's brother was quite rich; they owned a five-story apartment building. The Newari family who had offered me wood told them, "The lama is so poor that he lives in a house with rats. All the people, Nepalese and Tibetans alike, go to him for help – including the king! It is sad to see him living in such conditions. I promised to give him the lumber. But you are the lama's own relative, and you are quite rich, living in your own five-story house. How is it that you don't care about his situation?"

With everyone's help, then, I was able to build the house I presently live in. The wood seller, Chandra Sowu, provided me with 130,000 rupees' worth of wood. The Kagyu lama, Tenphel Gyaltsen, offered me 100,000 rupees' worth of bricks. Lhudrup Dorje donated iron worth 50,000 rupees. The Khampa, Dechen Tsomo, offered 55,000 rupees to buy cement. A top floor temple was built thanks to Tenzin-la, who contributed some 100,000 bags of cement. Additionally, a Swiss man named Rudolf, whom I had previously helped recover from depression, offered me a Guru Rinpoche statue worth 130,000 rupees. Other statues, including an Avalokiteshvara worth 100,000 rupees and Tara worth 100,000 rupees, were offered by a German man named Casting. With these statues, my house became like a monastery, and every month now I perform public pujas at my home. Before, I had neither house nor monastery. Now I have both rolled into one.

Illness and Recovery

Perhaps it was because I had been engaged in so many different activities for so long, but one day I had a stroke and became paralyzed on my right side. At the time, I was going to many pujas and working without a break almost every day. One day, I attended a wedding to give blessings to the married couple. A young woman offered me tea, but I declined. She was slightly offended, she and insisted that I take it. Suddenly, I felt pain in my right arm and right leg.

Much to her chagrin, I excused myself and went home to rest. But by the time I got home, I could not move the right side of my body at all. I just fell asleep, hoping it would be better. When I woke up, though, nothing on the right side would move at all. Even my mouth was limp on the right side.

Some friends of mine took me to see Chatral Rinpoche. "This is a very serious illness," he said, "and recovering from it will not be easy." He gave me blessings.

Then I was taken to see Ugyen Tulku at his retreat house at Nagi Gompa. Ugyen Tulku took a long and serious look at me when I arrived. "What is wrong, Lama?"

I told him I was paralyzed on my right side. "You are not someone to get ill," he said. "What happened?" Ugyen Tulku came over to me and put medicine on five places on my head, then along the right side of my arm, and my mouth. "You will heal," he said. "Stay with me at Nagi Gompa for a while. The nuns will take care of you."

So I stayed there for 15 days. Every day I received a massage on the right side of my body. Ugyen Tulku gave me and some other people the initiation and empowerment for the Longchen Nyingthig. Though there were many high lamas and Tulkus there, and Ugyen Tulku insisted that I sit right next to him at the front of the room. This was the fourth time that I had received the Longchen Nyingthig empowerment.

On the tenth day of the Tibetan month, he gave the empowerment for Milarepa. The nuns made a big batch of nettle soup, which is what Milarepa drank and why he is depicted as green. Tulku Ugyen approached me. "Today is Mila's empowerment, and the nettle soup will be distributed. Will you please serve it to all the people?"

I was very honored to participate in this. Everyone chanted this prayer for Mila: "JeMila Shepa, Dorje la, solwa depsol." It was so beautiful, with so many people chanting this in a beautiful melody. After the first 200 people were served, though, my back began to really hurt me. I set down the bowl of soup – and suddenly I stood right up. My back cracked loudly, and I started to get feeling back in my right side.

That night I fell into a deep sleep, and when I woke up, my roommate was shocked. He exclaimed, "Lama! Look! Your mouth isn't crooked any more!"

The Tibetans I had met there gave me a white belt to support my back, and soon I was walking all over the place. I even took a long walk up the mountain behind Nagi Gompa. I stayed for another two days before heading back home to Jawlayel. My friends were very happy to see me healthy again.

I couldn't wait to see Chatral Rinpoche and let him know that I was healed. He was shocked. "How on earth did you heal so fast?!"

In jest I told him, "I sang a song from Kham and it made me better." Interested now, Chatral Rinphoche wanted to know, "What song was that?"

"When looking at the vast plain, all the people come to sing 'Ala la,' and when you find yourself on a rocky road, remember Guru Rinpoche."

"Oh my!" he said. "And can you use your drum now?"

"Yes, of course."

"That is wonderful! Let's have some tea and a chat," he said.

I stayed with him for a few days and Chatral Rinpoche privately gave me the empowerment for Tangtong Gyalpo.

I had a cousin, a nun, who also helped me during my illness. She thought that as I got older, I would need some help. So she told me that because my son had several children in Tibet, it would be a good opportunity for them if I had them come to Nepal – they could get an education and, at the same time, be able to help me out. So she sent a message to my son, telling him about her idea. He agreed, and sent his two granddaughters, Yangzum and Dechen.

Later, when I was staying in retreat in Parping, Nepal, I one day vomited a little blood. I went to see a physician, but he didn't know what it was, so I went to an Indian doctor. This doctor couldn't help either, so I went to see a Newari doctor. He also didn't know what to do. He suggested a Brahmin doctor. The Brahmin doctor said I had lung disease and that I needed an x-ray. They did the x-ray and then sent me to the King's personal doctor. He told me that the other doctors had thought that I had lung cancer. And he asked me, "Do you sing?"

"I don't sing, but I do chant in pujas. Sometimes it's like shouting or like singing."

"How many years have you done this?"

"For forty years."

"Oh, this must be the cause," he said. "Your chanting has caused injuries in your lungs. You need to go to Bombay to get an operation. It appears that you have just three months to live."

The businessman Mr. Casting said that if I went to Bombay for the surgery, he would give me 100,000 India rupees to pay for it.

I had never been bad to other people, and yet here I was sick. I had practiced a lot, and I wasn't afraid to die. If I was going to die, though, I wanted to be in a holy place. What to do?

I went to Chatral Rinpoche for a divination. I explained to him what the doctors had told me. "Should I go to Bombay for an operation?" I asked.

"With trust in Guru Rinpoche you will have a long life," he replied. I immediately went to Parping to start a retreat. I stayed in a room near the Vajrayogini temple doing prayers for nine months. My granddaughter cared for me the whole time. After the retreat, I recovered very well.

During my retreat, the refugees, thinking of how I had helped them so much over the years, did pujas for me. They didn't want me to die. The old people especially prayed for me not to leave them. "Of all the people, Lama Wangdu should be protected," they prayed. They did a special Tara puja for me one day. Some even brought me presents while I stayed in Parping. In the end I was completely cured of any illness.

I think my physician was later embarrassed about not being able to help me, because he gave me gifts for the Nepalese New Year that year.

One day a Tibetan woman died and I went to the hospital for the Powa. In the hospital I met the doctor who had originally diagnosed me with cancer.

"My God! Where have you come from?" he exclaimed. He was very surprised to see me. He invited me to his home. "I feel a little embarrassed at not being able to cure you," he confessed.

I explained to him, "You did me a great favor. From you I came to learn of my disease. You are indeed my teacher. If you hadn't diagnosed me, I would have stayed in Jawalakhel unaware, going here and there. I wouldn't have been able to go on retreat and heal. You indeed saved my life."

House in Parping

There was a landlord of a house in Parping who planned to live upstairs in his building while monks would live below. He built himself a small room on the roof. However, when the landlord had finished the house, he died of a stroke. His son, Pema Puntsok, was saddened by his father's death. "Our poor father worked so hard to build a retreat center," he said. "And he wasn't able to stay there even one day."

Dechen Tsomo, the Khampa, said, "Our lama is living in Parping and paying for rent. Is it possible for him to stay in your house?"

"Lama is like our own father," said the sons. "He always does pujas for us. Of course it's okay for him to live here."

I moved in immediately. If visitors came to see me and it rained, we all got wet on the roof and had to hurry inside. During the day, people would get sunburned. One nun brought me a blue canvas to put up over my room as a shelter. When it rained or when it was windy, the tarp made a lot of noise.

One day a woman named Sang Palmo came for a divination. She said, "If you had a tin roof, you will be protected from the wind and rain. I will put one up for you." And soon she came in a pickup truck filled with tin sheets. "We had extra tin," she said, "so we will make you a roof." A Nepalese workman put up the poles and roof in just one day, and I put up some fabric walls.

One day a strong wind blew away all the fabric walls. The nuns who lived below put up all kinds of things – clothing, blankets, and plastic – to replace them. When visitors tried to find me in Parping, people would tell them, "He's very easy to find; he lives between the Tara cave and the Vajrayogini temple. He has a tin roof that is covered with cloth scraps and plastic as windows."

But I said, "It doesn't matter. In the past, great masters such as Padampa Sangye, Jigme Lingpa, and Milarepa lived in caves or under trees with only a small blanket. They ate the leftovers at funeral sites, and they wore the clothes left from the dead. We already have too much comfort. We are like insects compared to them. For me, living here is not a problem."

"Although it may be spiritually correct to say this," they responded, "we feel sad seeing our lama living this way." Many people wanted to offer me things to improve my living quarters.

The nuns told the landlords that although I was happy, the room looked really ugly. People walked by and looked at the plastics blowing around, and tourists were even taking pictures of it. The landlord finally decided to put up glass windows.

Kalachakra Blessings

In 1972, the Dalai Lama gave the Kalachakra initiation in bodhgaya, and 300,000 people were in attendance. Among those present was Yongzen Ling Rinpoche, who offered the initiation for Trakpo Sum Dil. Ling Rinpoche's secretary met with me personally and offered me a sacred cake and chang – personally from Ling Rinpoche. Then he asked me to help them distribute things to the people during the ceremony. I was very pleased to be able to participate.

There is a holy place about six hours' drive southeast of Bodhgaya, where a peach once fell on my head when I was sitting under a tree. I considered this a special blessing, and I dried the peach and put it inside my Guru Rinpoche statue at home. Twelve years later, I was building a new Guru statue, and I took out the special things from inside my old statue to give to Chatral Rinpoche, who was placing them inside the new statue. When I gave the dried fruit to Chatral Rinpoche he asked, "What is this thing?"

"When I was in Bodhgaya, it fell on my head. I've kept it inside my Guru statue at home ever since."

Chatral Rinpoche put the shriveled fruit to his head to honor it, and just then some juice came out of it. He captured the juice in his hands and drank it. He then exclaimed that this fruit was a blessing from Dzambala, the god of abundance. The image of Dzambala actually shows him holding a peach. Chatral Rinpoche was very happy with this offering! I still have this statue in my shrine in Nepal.

Statues to Tibet

Over the years, I learned that Padampa's monastery in Langkor had been defaced and the statues of Padampa Sangye, Milarepa, and Tangtong Gyalpo with stolen or destroyed. I had such fond memories of the temple and felt I needed to do something about this. So in 1992 I began raising money to have these statues remade and sent back to the monastery in Langkor. Six years later, I finally had three statues made: Dampa Sangye's statue was gold-plated and cost about 375,000 rupees. The statues of Milarepa and Tangtong Gyalpo each cost 100,000 rupees. I bought silver offering bowls costing 50,000 rupees, along with drums, cymbals, and other religious objects – a total purchase of 775,000 rupees. I then did 100,000 tsok offerings and sent all these objects to Tibet.

The Chinese granted permission to the Tingri Tibetans to bring the statues back, and the lama from Langkor and one Chinese official came to the border to receive the statues. I had acquired the necessary permission from the Archaeology Department in Nepal to take the statues out. I packed the statues in boxes in preparation for the trip.

On the morning that I was preparing for the trip, though, some helpers were loading the truck when some people shouted, "A monkey got into your Shrine room."

"There are no monkeys in Jawalakhel," I replied. "How can there be a monkey in my room?" I quickly went up there to see for myself.

Indeed, there was a big black monkey with a white beard sitting there with the statues. I was very confused. I thought it might be an obstacle for the statues at the border, or perhaps there would be an accident with the car. I looked at the statue of Guru Rinpoche to see whether the obstacles might arise in my mind, and immediately I remembered that Dhampa Sangye was supposed to have a monkey face. I felt comforted then, as I realized that this was not an obstacle but actually an emanation of Dhampa Sangye.

I then went to find bananas, and I took a dozen of them to the monkey. When I came to him with the bananas, the monkey climbed down from the statue of Padampa and stood on the boxes that the other statues were packed in. The monkey was looking right at me as if he had something to say. With bananas in hand I said to him, "Milarepa, Tangtong Gyalpo, and Dampa Sangye, I'm trying to see you three off to Tibet. I'm wishing that the sun of happiness will soon shine on the world. Please help them go to Tibet."

I then offered the bananas to the monkey. Taking them from me, he climbed up the stairs and sat down. He set two bananas at his right side, and he started to peel one. He looked at me with happiness. I then began to feel relieved and comfortable. This was not, after all, an obstacle; this was a miracle from the Mahasiddhas.

I then packed everything into the car for the trip. As I was doing this, though, at one point a big red dog came and blocked my path. It seemed to be saying that I shouldn't go, so I again felt doubtful about this endeavor. I asked a Tibetan friend in the car, "A dog got in my way; what does this mean?"

"It seemed to say that you should indeed send the statues to Tibet, but that you shouldn't go yourself." And so I got into the car with both doubt and happiness in my heart.

Normally, the trip to the Tibet border in Nepal is blocked with bamboo crossbeams at each of the check posts. This time, though, we were never stopped or even asked questions. The driver was surprised. "Normally the cars are questioned at the checkpoints," he said. "This is very strange. They didn't even ask us one question, and they just let us pass by!"

When we reached the border, the Nepalese police asked what was inside the car. I showed them the certificate issued by the Archaeology Department. "There are many statues and copper," they said. "What is all this for?"

The driver answered, "An old lama is going to take these things to a monastery in Tibet."

"Are these objects for doing pujas? When is this lama going to do a puja for me?"

"This is a poor lama," replied my driver. "He doesn't have enough money to do a puja for you. How much puja do you need?"

"I need 3,000 rupees for my puja," answered the policeman.

"He doesn't have any money," said the driver. "But instead I'll give you 1,500 rupees."

And with that they agreed to let the car pass the border.

We met the people who had come to escort the statues, and we presented them with a special poem which declared:

> I am the son of the Penak family.
> I have been in Nepal a long time.
> Whatever money I made doing pujas, I have used to make these statues,
> And I am handing them over to the Langkor monastery of

Dhampa Sangye,

On the fourteenth day of the eleventh month of the Tibetan calendar in the western year of 1998.

When I handed over the statues and other items to the lama from Langkor, he broke into tears. I told him, "Because of karmic connections, you were born in Langkor. As it is said in the texts, you are one of those lucky to be born in sacred places. You should take care of the monastery. Don't think about making money for yourself. If I can, I will send you money from Nepal." They then offered me chang and meat from Tibet.

The statues reached Langkor on the fifteenth, the full moon day. On the sixteenth, they arranged the statues properly, and dressed them and did blessings. On the seventeenth they invited all the Langkor villagers; 515 people came to view the statues. They gave each person one of the black protection cords I had sent. The people wondered, "Who is this Wangdu who sent such a wonderful offering to our village?"

Many young Tibetans then wanted to see me. They wrote to me, "If you are able to live long enough, please visit us in Langkor, just one time."

Although I have not been able to go back there since I left in 1958, their invitations have caused my thoughts to move back again to my birthplace.

Swami

In 1998 I met an American named Swami Ji. He said he practiced Hinduism, but that he also liked the practices of Milarepa, Dampa

Sangye, and other secluded Buddhist ascetics. He had asked someone whether there were any yogis in Nepal, and they brought him to me. When I met him, he asked me what my ascetic practice was. "I was born in the village where Dampa Sangye's monastery was established," I told him. "I take Dhampa Sangye's tradition as my main practice."

"What practices are involved with that?" he asked.

"Mostly we practice Chöd."

He asked me to perform Chöd for him. He appreciated the practice very much and he expressed his interest to learn it slowly. Swami then asked me to perform Chöd at a funeral site, so I went to Pashupatinath two times to do the Chöd ritual and dances. I also performed Chöd at a funeral site called Ramadole.

I had performed Chöd at Ramadole another time with Chatral Rinpoche and his monks.

Swami then asked me, "I heard there is a sacred place where you can pray to Guru Rinpoche for a long life. Can you go there to do this puja for us?" So then twenty-five Americans and five Tibetans flew by helicopter to the site; we stayed for five days for the ceremony.

"Your practices of Padampa Sangye, your healing, mantra, and Powa practices are very profound and wise," he told me. But now you are 63 years old. You might live another 15 years. If you can teach young Tibetans now, they would be able to continue the traditions. If your students become experts, they will be able to teach in America. You should teach to those with good English, those who are above the high school level. I will support this project. We will sponsor three or four such young Tibetans."

I then thought very deeply about Swami Ji's suggestion about finding a young Tibetan to teach Padampa Sangye's tradition.

Other Offers

One day a man named Tsering Thundrup came to me accompanied by a German man. "We have a Dharma center in Germany," they said. "We would like you to come this year to teach. Please make the documents quickly."

I refused. "Right now I am not physically fit to travel."

At about the same time, some Taiwanese came and asked me to visit Taiwan as soon as I could. "I don't know the language," I said. "I don't have a translator and I don't have travel documents. It isn't possible for me to come." So again I refused.

Meeting His Holiness the Dalai Lama

In 1999 I came to Portland, Oregon, to stay with Swami-Ji's Ashram for a few months. Yangzum, my oldest grandaughter, came with me, and Swami offered to send her to school so that she could learn English. My other granddaughter Dechen came back from India to stay with me in the U.S. and help me out.

I went to Indiana to attend His Holiness the Dalai Lama's Kalachakra. When I came back to Oregon, 300 people showed up at Swami-Ji's Ashram to receive the Chöd initiation and empowerments, and the teaching on Powa, the Transference of Consciousness, from me. I stayed in the U.S. for six months, and by the end of my time there, more than 100 people were able to proficiently perform the Chöd ritual and dance.

The next year, when I came back to America, His Holiness the Dalai Lama was in Portland giving teachings. There in Portland, he and I met privately. He spent three hours with me, talking about my life story and my main practices. He gave me a beautiful statue of the thousand-armed Chenrezig, and he invited me to Dharamsala for another private audience.

When I returned to Nepal, I organized a team of 73 people to come to Dharamsala with me in buses. We all made a large tsok offering at the parade grounds near His Holiness's residence. He called for me and said, "Padampa Sangye has no community of practitioners. It's important that you establish one for the tradition." He offered me an antique 15-inch Buddha statue. He also gave me 1,600,000 rupees (about $23,300) and an official letter from his office approving donations for this project.

Following that, we went to Tso-pema to offer a large Tsok. We gave seven large bags of biscuits to the fish in the lake. The next day, we couldn't see any fish. Concerned, we inquired about where the fish had gone. A local told us that the fish sleep after they eat a lot. Not to worry, he said, they will be fine.

There were only a few Bedong islands in the lake this time, and all of them came over to us while we were performing the ceremony. Above the lake are very special Guru Rinpoche caves where nuns live, and we also did a large tsok there. We gave 26,000 rupees to all the nuns who lived there – about 75 of them. They treated us kindly, offering tea and plenty to eat.

A local lama, called Lama Wangdur, was building a large Guru Rinpoche statue. I offered him 10,000 rupees for this project.

I met a woman practitioner who used to translate for and attend to Lama Kusum Lingpa. She had helped to build a replica of Boudanath stupa in Golok Tibet. After the stupa was finished, Kusum Lingpa asked her to stay at Tsopema on retreat for three years. I was walking around the lake with my granddaughter, and there was this woman standing on the balcony. She told us her story.

"I don't see anyone," she said. "I'm on strict retreat. However, let me ask you a question. Do you practice Padampa Sangye's tradition?"

"Yes, I do," I replied.

"In that case, please come inside and give me a teaching."

It turned out she had had a dream that Padampa Sangye was going to come to Tsopema the night before. I gave her the teaching of Guru Yoga for Padampa. She was very pleased. She told us that people, upon hearing that she was on retreat, would just spontaneously offer her money. It came from the U.S. every month, though she had never asked anyone for help.

Finally, we returned back to Nepal. With the letter from His Holiness the Dalai Lama, many people donated money to the project. I collected enough to buy a small deserted monastery nearby Boudhanath, where the old Shelkar monastery had been re-established in exile. The old man who lived in the monastery told us, "If anyone else wanted this, I'd sell it for more than 11 million rupees. Because it is you, though, and because you are from Shelkar, I will sell it for 8.5 million." It was a done deal!

I then had three statues made, each of which were more than six feet tall: Machig, Padampa Sangye, and Yeshe Tsogyal. The sponsors were Lhasa Sonam Lha, Babu Kaje, and Kerry Smith. I also had the 21

Taras made, each 18 inches tall, thanks to Geshe Sonam Gyatsen, who now lives in Japan. Dzambala, more than 36 inches tall, was courtesy of, Tsering La. The Mani wheel had two sponsors, Gonpe'i Jamyang and Kangjong Ngodrup. Many other people offered so much. The total cost for this was 2,500,000 rupees.

We now, in 2008, have nearly 25 monks here. For our monthly Tsok offerings, close to 50 people come to the monastery to participate. Two monks are from Lhasa, and 15 monks are already well versed in dharma. Five of the younger monks have no parents, and initially came to my monastery with no clothes to wear nor homes to go to.

One day a man with a young son came to visit. The boy must have been about four years old. They sat in my waiting room without saying a word. They came two different times, and each time I gave them five rupees. The young boy gave his money to his father. After two weeks, the father came again to give this child to the monastery to be a monk. The boy cried, but he said that he knew his father couldn't afford to take care of him.

The monastery has already been outgrown by the 25 monks in residence, and we are looking at expanding. Ideally, I would like to have 50 monks to help the poor families and orphaned children living in Nepal.

Mainly we teach the Perfection of Wisdom sutras, the teachings of Pacification from Padampa, and the Chöd from Machig Lapdron. At the core of our teachings is loving kindness to others. My monks are required to finish the 100,000 preliminary practices after completion of their academic studies. Only one monk has thus far reached this level. There are 21 monks who are just starting the practice. As long as they practice sincerely, they will have a place to stay and food to eat here in the monastery. As the monks advance in their practice, I will provide them with a solitary cave for more intense practice. It is my hope that one day, the monks, having finished their training, will travel the world teaching the tradition.

In this way, I have tried to follow the instructions of His Holiness.

Three Monks from China

One day, three lamas came from China to visit me. One was Shapkar's incarnation, one was Jang Kyamgon's incarnation, and one was the incarnation of Milarepa's famous disciple Rechung. They came to me to receive the transmission for Machig Lapdron and Padampa Sangye. In appreciation afterward, they wrote a prayer for me.

Originally, though they had come from China, where they were recognized as incarnations of high lamas, there was no more Dharma transmission for a spiritual lineage. So they visited the Dalai Lama, who suggested that they could receive the transmission of Chöd from me. They have since returned to China, and they have invited me to visit there. However, because of the political complications and controversy among Nepal, Tibet, and China, I have been unable to acquire a proper visa.

Here is a translation of their poem:

The compassionate Wisdom Body, king of all Victorious Ones,
Who embodies as one, the Indian, Holy Father (Padampa),
And the Great Mother from the Land of Snows, the Lamp for All (MaChik Labdron)
I pray you grant undying Wisdom.

Master holder of the practice lineage of the teachings of Shijé,
The supreme tulku from Tingri, Wangdu who overpowers all,
Through relying on you in all lifetimes till the end of samsara,
In order to benefit others, may the four activities be spontaneously
accomplished.

Death in New York City

In 2007 His Holiness the Dalai Lama called upon all the Nyingma lamas to visit him. I offered him a very fine Mandala, weighing 10.5 kilograms, full of gold, coral, turquoise, silver, and other precious items, along with two butter lamps of about 11 kilograms each. This offering was worth 2,500,000 rupees – well over $36,000. In return, he gave me three statues of Manitoba, White Tara, and Gold Tara for the Temple.

Later, when I returned to Nepal, I participated in the inauguration of the new Tamang Temple next to Boudhanath. This was sort of a goodbye for me, because I was about to leave for America once more.

So again I returned to Portland, Oregon. I performed a long life puja for the Tibetan people living there in Oregon. Next, I was invited to Tara Mandala, a beautiful mountain retreat center run by Tsultrim Alione in Colorado. There were about 45 people there who had come to receive the Chöd initiation and transmission. Tsultrim Alione's students asked me to write a prayer for her long life, and I very much enjoyed composing this for her. I had a wonderful time there and hope to return again.

In New York, a Tamang woman named Maya Tamang, originally from Nepal, was very sick. She invited me to New York for a puja. She told me, "You've helped our family for many years. Now that I'm in the United States, I have to have a lama to help me. Would you come to visit me in New York? I am unable to travel."

This woman's mother called me from Nepal, asking for many divinations, and she cried many times. One Mr. Ugyen from the Tamang community sponsored my trip to New York. I visited her three times in the hospital; I gave her the Padampa Sangye mantra and healing salt. And after a week or so, she died. I was honored to be a part of the funeral ceremony, and her body was sent to Nepal for cremation. The Tamang community then asked me to stay and give empowerments. I stayed for a month before returning to the West Coast.

It was then that I had the good fortune of meeting His Holiness the Dalai Lama for the fourth time in my life; it was in Seattle during the Kalachakra initiation. Some 50,000 people attended for the main ceremony, and then there was a special meeting just for Tibetans. After this I was invited to His Holiness's room for a private audience.

After that I spent several months putting together and doing practice for 50 ceremonial vases for long life and abundance. I decided to offer these to Swami for his birthday, and then return to Kathmandu.

Puja

In order to show gratitude to my family, on every tenth and twenty-fifth day of the Tibetan month, I offer Chöd tsok. This tradition comes from when I was growing up in Langkor. Also on the fourth day of the sixth month, when the Buddha first began teaching the Dharma, I offer 100,000 tsok in Boudha. I also donate money to paint the stupa there and change its dressings.

These days I do divinations for marriage, and I heal sicknesses for people on request.

This is my story until now.

Colophon

In the western year 1998, in Kathmandu Nepal, I met Ngawang Kalden (Joshua Waldman) and Thinley Thundrup, who wanted to write the story of my activities – in autobiography form. Since this story has started, many people have complimented it as a good project. Others wanted this to happen before, but were unable to carry it out.

"Kalden Ley Dro Chen" means "auspicious connection," so Ngawang Kalden therefore somehow has an auspicious connection with my life story – and the interpreter, Thinley, whose name means "enlightened activity which goes beyond the universe," will indeed benefit limitless beings beyond the universe.

I have enjoyed telling as much as I can remember of my life. If you can write this as a book in English and Tibetan, I told them, then people will gain trust and faith in the Dharma – and will benefit greatly. To those who do not have faith in the Dharma, those who have wrong views, who are jealous or simple-minded – my biography might be of little use. Whatever the case may be, though, these are the stories of my crazy wisdom yogic lifestyle, which are like a blooming lotus flower.

Teaching on POWA

T his chapter will discuss the method for the transference of consciousness, or *Powa*: how to do it, when to do it, and what to visualize[1]. This tradition is rooted in the Dzogchen Longchen Nyingthig – heart essence of Longchenpa. When one is training and practicing to do *Powa*, there are detailed visualizations involved, but when one is doing it for others, when others are dying, we can substitute the the recitation of mantras instead of the detailed visualizations.

The name of this practice – transference of consciousness – is often called enlightenment without meditation, which means it is very easy to do and very effective in bringing about liberation. The only qualifications necessary are faith and confidence. Even the prayer to be recited is only nine lines. It is worth mentioning that those extraordinary individuals who have mastered the six perfections, including the perfection of wisdom, have no need to do Powa, because they understand that there is nothing to be transferred. These individuals have realized emptiness, the nature of all phenomena, and the nature of the mind. This, then, could be called the ultimate, or highest, level of Powa.

---

[1] The text for this practice can be found at:
http://www.mahasiddha.org/store/Texts.html

For those of us who don't have such realizations, but still have faith and confidence, we learn Powa so we can transfer our consciousness to the pure realms. For sentient beings who cannot recite the mantras (such as cows, dogs, monkeys and other creatures), we can help by doing the visualizations and transferring their consciousness for them. Similarly, when we have such faith and confidence, whenever we see any dead beings, even in documentaries, films or in the news, or when we see the loss of lives in catastrophes, we can simply visualize and recite the nine-line mantra and perform the transference of their consciousness. In this way we can help liberate individuals from an ordinary state to the pure realm of Amitabha Buddha.

If one practices for others with love and compassion, with pure motivation for their sake, this practitioner will be blessed by the Buddhas and Bodhisattvas and all the other divine beings. As a result, that compassionate person will always have a positive life, free from unfavorable circumstances, and will enjoy longevity, benefiting both others and self on the path to enlightenment.

The term "Powa" in Tibetan means "transference from an ordinary state to a superior or better state of being." In this present life, one has this body and consciousness, this crude ordinary self. But after death, Powa can transfer our consciousness to the pure realm called Mahasukhavati, or the Blissful Pure Land of Amitabha Buddha. From there we can more easily attain perfect enlightenment.

The practice of Powa for the sake of others consists of guiding the dead person's consciousness onto a right path. For example, a horseman may be galloping toward a cliff where he is in danger of falling. If he is guided to a safe place before he reaches the edge of the cliff, then he can be saved. In the same way, with compassion, we can guide the bewildered mind of the dead person away from falling into a state of suffering, liberating that person to the pure land through the practice of Powa.

However, learning about the methods of Powa by itself is not sufficient. One should truly have the power to transfer consciousness. And that power is obtained from one's confidence and faith in the practice and in the power of Buddha Amitabha. Furthermore, this ability is rooted in our faith and devotion toward the lamas of the lineage from whom we have received these teachings and instructions, supported by the foundation of love and compassion.

Depending on different cultures and religions, there are different ways of disposing of the dead. For example, some bury their dead in a coffin, whereas Buddhists and Hindus cremate them. In the Buddhist point of view, within the body we enshrine a hundred different deities, 42 in the heart and 58 in the head. When we die, if the consciousness is not transferred and the body is cremated or buried, you are literally burying or cremating all the deities that reside within. However, if you transfer the consciousness to the pure realm before burial or cremation, then you are just disposing of a body which is nothing more than its elemental substances; earth to earth, water to water.

How to Perform Powa for Others

Practicing generosity, being kind and compassionate, as well as teaching dharma, will benefit others greatly. Yet with Powa, we are able to help those who have died, without having to know anything about their minds or circumstances of their lives. There is great merit in helping to transfer them to the pure realms and thus avoid their rebirth in lower realms of existence.

When one dies, the consciousness wanders alone with no self-control, like a leaf in the wind, guided only by one's own karma. There is no refuge on which to rely. If an ordinary person dies without any knowledge about their consciousness, or life after death, there is a lot of suffering and confusion. When they die they suddenly find themselves completely alone, with nothing to rely on. Even for great people such as kings, ministers, or wealthy persons – when they die, none of the power or wealth they had before will help them. They all have to travel alone in the afterlife, equally lost without any knowledge of where to go or what will happen. The practice of Powa can guide them through this time of confusion and bewilderment to a pure path, to a definite destination. One should keep in mind how very effective and beneficial this practice can be for others.

There is one thing which is very certain: whoever has taken birth will surely die one day. Whether rich or poor, young or old, everyone has to face death. There are no exceptions. The way we are born is the same, but how we die is different. Some die of old age, some die an untimely death under unfavorable circumstances or misfortune. Some die suddenly; some linger on in pain for a long time.

By remembering and thinking constantly of the certainty of death and the uncertainty of its occurrence, we will know that there is no avoiding death. Yet just by remembering this, it can help us to prepare for what will happen after death. Now is the time to for you to gather provisions for future lives.

Holy beings such as Buddhas, bodhisattvas, and great lamas have no other intention than to benefit beings. One way they strive to do this is in teaching us how to face death, and in bringing us to better circumstances after death. Through skillful means and wisdom, they teach us methods on how to have a long and happy life, and how to be free from unfavorable circumstances such as illness, poverty, and other kinds of suffering. But one of the most important teachings is the one that shows us the way after this life, after our death. Thus the instructions on the path of Powa are among the most important.

It is very important to teach older people the transference of consciousness while they are still alive.

We have this physical body composed of the different elements. For example, our blood is the water element, bone and flesh are the earth element, heat is the fire element, breath is the wind element, and consciousness is the element of space. These elements come together to form our body when we are born, and we then grow like a tree. But when our growth reaches its limit, it has to decline.

Suppose someone has reached the age of 90 and the physical body is then declining. You can see indications when death is approaching. At this point, no matter how much medication one takes, no matter how many prayers and pujas are performed, nothing will prolong life or stop the person from dying. The approach of death will be evident when indications manifest that the five elements are dismantling inside of a person.

First, the water element will dissolve into the earth element. This is indicated by dryness, whereby fluids in the body such as saliva and other bodily secretions diminish. In the next stage, the earth element dissolves into the fire element, resulting in a feeling of heaviness in the body, and stiffness or loss of flexibility. Next, the fire element dissolves into the wind element. This will cause a person to feel cold, and any part of the body will also feel cold to the touch. Then the wind element dissolves into the space element.

In the human body, there are 21,000 types of wind energy that flow in our system and are responsible for different functions. For example, the downward flowing wind energy is responsible for urination and other secretions, while the upward flowing wind is related to speaking, coughing, breathing, and so on. So the indication that the wind element is dissolving into the space element is that our breathing become labored – hard, loud, and faster. Exhalation and inhalation become short and brief. When all 21,000 types of the wind element dissolve into space, the body becomes placid and still, and from a medical point of view we are considered dead. This is called the moment of death.

However, at this moment in the heart chakra, there remains the white energy that is responsible for life. Even though at this point the body has stopped breathing and is seen as physically dead, the inner energy of the life-force still resides. The sign of the inner life-force finally departing depends on the individual. For some, after the final physical breath, there is a pause before a final exhalation occurs; sometimes there is some other indication. When that occurs, it means the inner consciousness, the energy within the heart, has departed.

So at the moment of death, the person will experience a blackout from the physical world, but the consciousness still resides within the heart center. The awareness becomes quite dull, with no feelings of pain or suffering. The experience is like some kind of profound quietness. This is the exact moment that one should practice Powa for them. This is the critical point at which one should help by guiding the consciousness.

It is important to keep the environment around a dying person peaceful and serene. We should avoid being sad, crying loudly, or making emotional outbursts in their presence. Whoever is performing the Powa should tell the dead, "Now you have died, which is nothing unusual. Everyone dies, so do not worry. You are not the only one. Everyone who is born must go through this, and now your moment has arrived. Because you have now died, your consciousness has separated from your body. Do not be attached to your parents, spouse, children, wealth, fame, or anything from your old life. Let go of all attachments and grasping. Keep yourself alert and aware – and have confidence, for I am going to deliver you to the pure land of Buddha Amitabha by Powa. Have confidence and you will be transferred to the pure land which is superior to what you are leaving behind. From there you can reach perfect enlightenment." You should speak like this when doing the Powa for the departed.

The Method

To perform Powa, you must generate a genuine and immeasurable compassion for the dead person. You must also have devotion, confidence, and faith in Buddha Amitabha, as well as confidence in the method. All this is essential.

First, we do Powa viewing the dead body not in its ordinary form, but in the form of Vajrayogini, and that the corpse transforms instantly into Vajrayogini. Vajrayogini is a semi-wrathful female deity, red in color. Wearing bone ornaments, her left hand holds a skullcup filled with blood, and her right hand holds a curved knife. She has three eyes that gaze upward longingly. The blood in the skullcup symbolizes the four maras: the mara of death, the mara of afflictions, the mara of aggregates, and Mara of arrogance. The curved knife symbolizes the cutting of the root of attachment. Her three eyes gazing upward symbolize longing to be in Amitabha's pure land, concentrated there and not distracted elsewhere. Her body is red and a little transparent, so you can see through it just a little.

We also visualize the central channel running from the lower part of the body to the top of the head, like a bamboo. This is like a pillar in the middle of the house. From the bottom to the top of the central channel, it is free from any obstacles, very straight, clear and luminous. The wall is as thin as a lotus petal, and the stem is straight like the stem of a lotus growing in the water. It is luminous like the flame of a sesame oil lamp, which is clearer and more luminous than other types of oil lamp flames. The channel at the bottom is narrower, while at the crown it flares like the mouth of a bell. At the heart center, you should visualize a pea-sized sphere, a drop that is green in color; this is the essence of our consciousness. This pea-sized representation of our consciousness is not still, but should be seen as vibrating and alive. In the middle of the green and vibrant pea-sized drop, we visualize the white sphere of the vital force in the form of a white letter HRI which symbolizes our awareness.

This HRI is not still; it flutters like a flag on a roof in the breeze.

Thus we visualize the dead in the form of a translucent red Vajrayogini, with the central channel that is like a luminous pipe, and the pea-sized green drop in the heart chakra containing the vibrant white HRI We should practice so that we can visualize all this in an instant. With some practice, it will come easily.

In general we have nine apertures in our body. When we do Powa, we should visualize these nine doors or apertures as blocked, because if the consciousness exits through any one of these nine doors, it will result in rebirth in one of the six realms, or in the lower realms. We need to block these nine doors and visually open a new one, which is the Brahmanical aperture at the top of the head.

Having rapidly visualized all this in detail, the next visualization is accompanied by the recitation of a prayer to Buddha Amitabha. Visualize Buddha Amitabha at the height of one arm's length above the head of the person for whom the Powa is being performed, whether it is oneself or the deceased. In the heart of Buddha Amitabha rests a lotus flower with a moon disc. In the center of the disc is the letter HRI surrounded by the mantra Om Ami Dewa Hri, all white in color. Remember that Buddha Amitabha is constantly gazing upon sentient beings with great compassion, wishing to deliver them from their ordinary states to rebirth in his pure land, Mahasukhavati, the Pure Land of Bliss.

Having visualized all this vividly and in detail, and having recited the nine-line prayer, you now pronounce the syllable HRI five times. Your tongue touches the upper back gums when you pronounce the HRI. Each time HRI is pronounced, the pea-sized drop vibrates more and more intensely, and rises higher and higher until it reaches the top of the head. When the drop has reached the crown of the head, at that moment shout as loudly and forcefully as you can the syllable HIK and visualize that the consciousness is ejected out and into the heart of Buddha Amitabha, much like a person shooting an arrow straight up. You need to repeat this sequence a total of three times[2].

When you do Powa for the dead, you may also consider that you are doing it for everyone else who may have died at that moment at

---

[2] The Melody as performed by Lama Wangdu can be downloaded at www.lamawangdu.org/powa.html

other locations. Visualize all of them together flying like a flock of birds in a field when they are startled by a sudden noise. So in the same way, the consciousness of all who have died at that time are liberated to the realm of Buddha Amitabha. An immeasurable amount of merit is thus accumulated by the person for whom Powa is being performed. This is because he has become the cause for you to perform Powa for many other people as well, and has thus played a role in liberating them all. The person performing Powa has also accumulated immense merit and benefit. In this way the consciousness of the dead are transferred to a pure realm.

After delivering the consciousness, it is time to deliver the buddha essence of the elements. This is done by rapidly pronouncing the syllable PHAT five times. The divinities in the heart and the essence of five elements are essentially the five primordial Buddhas. The red fire element is Amitabha, the yellow earth element is Ratnasambhava, and so on. Each of these are transferred into the heart of Buddha Amitabha with the utterance of PHAT, and Amitaba lets them in to the pure realm Mahasukhavati.

Self-Liberation

When practicing Powa for yourself, you need to keep your body straight, so that the central channel will be straight, and the inner wind energies can then flow freely. If the wind energy is without obstruction, then the mind becomes clear and free. When the mind is clear, then concentration and visualization are vivid. This is how they are interconnected.

When practicing Powa on yourself, there are some differences in the technique; after all, you are not dead! The visualization of the central channel, the vibrant green pea-sized drop with a red HRI, and Buddha Amitabha above one's head are all identical. However in this case, you visualize yourself in your ordinary form and not as Vajrayogini.

After you perform the ejection of consciousness into Amitabha's heart, you need to return your consciousness back into your own body. This also acts as a long-life practice, because doing Powa repeatedly can loosen the bond between mind and body, and thereby shorten one's life. Thus the following practice can assure that your life will be long and your Powa practice is balanced and healthful during this life.

After you do the HRI, HRI, HIK pattern and dissolve into Buddha Amitabha's heart, you need to perform the dissolution of Amitabha into your own body. You should think that Amitabha is the essence of your root guru, and above him are the lineage gurus all the way up to Vajradhara. After ejecting your consciousness, the blessings of the lineage from the Vajradhara come down through your root guru in the form of Buddha Amitabha. To Amitaba's right is Chenrezig, and to his left is Vajrapani, his two regents. They also dissolve into light and dissolve into him. Amitabha becomes smaller in size and then enters your brahma aperture at the top of your head, continuing down to your heart chakra to rest on an eight-petaled red lotus, where he remains.

That Amitabha Buddha, the essence of all gurus of lineage and Buddhas and bodhisattvas, is sitting in your heart chakra on a ruby-red lotus. The lotus petals close around him and enshrine him, creating a luminous glass-like flame inside. Keep this in your heart.

Through the power of this visualization and the power of your attitude, your ordinary self transforms into Buddha Amitayus, the Buddha of infinite life. Amitayus is the essence of Buddha Amitabha, but manifesting with a crown and a vase of long life with the nectar of immortality. Recite the mantra of Amitayus, which is OM AMARANI ZEWAN TEYE SOHA, as many times as possible.

Through this practice you will have a life free of negativity, worry, mental suffering, physical illness, or disease. Any being who practices this kind of meditation will have an immense impact on others. Whoever sees, hears, or touches such a person will always feel joy and happiness, and will receive blessings from them.

Memorize the nine line prayer of Powa, so that whenever you see anyone dead or hear of people dying or being killed, you can visualize the mantra and pray strongly for them to be liberated in Buddha Amitabha's pure realm. Even if you accidentally kill an insect, transfer its consciousness. When in a restaurant eating chicken, beef, or other meat, you can recite the mantras before eating and visualize the consciousness of those beings, whose meat you are about to consume, being transferred to the pure realm. When you eat meat, think with compassion, "May the negativity of that being be purified, and the negativity of consuming that being be purified."

When you are eating or drinking, don't think you are doing so for your own pleasure and satisfaction. Rather, adopt the attitude that you are making offerings to all the deities you have enshrined in your heart chakra, to Buddha Amitabha and the other holy beings.

If you make such offerings when eating rice, meat, vegetables, and so on, everyone involved in cultivating and producing that meal will accumulate positive merit, and any negativity incurred in that production is purified. With this positive attitude, you help everyone who contributed to that meal's production.

When the meal is finished and you are happy, you should then think, "I am so lucky to have had such a delicious meal. May everyone have such an experience, and may everyone in the world be free from hunger." Whatever you don't finish eating, don't dispose of it as trash. Rather, you should dispose of it with the compassionate attitude that regards it as offerings to beings who are unfortunate and don't have food. Make offerings to them so that they benefit from it. Thus you should make offerings to the Buddhas and bodhisattvas before eating, and then offer the leftovers to less fortunate beings who are in need.

As humans, we are intelligent, sensible beings with some spiritual understanding. We cherish the spiritual path, so we should practice and lead our life in a spiritual way even while we eat, drink, or sleep. Think of all our activities in life as Dharma practice. When we make the best use of our precious human lives for the maximum benefit of both ourselves and others, we separate ourselves from simple animals. A cow just eats and sleeps without any idea of such things; we can do better.

Questions & Answers

Question: The texts say to visualize ourselves as Vajrayogini, but your instructions say to visualize ourselves in our ordinary form. Which way should it be practiced?

Lama Wangdu: When you do the practice of Powa for someone already dead, then that person should be visualized as Vajrayogini no matter what. But if doing it for yourself, you can visualize yourself in your ordinary form. If you are an experienced practitioner, you can visualize yourself in the form of Vajrayogini. These are different choices based on your ability and experience.

Question: Would you talk more about the importance of the nine line prayer for Powa?

Lama Wangdu: When you get to the third line of the prayer which reads, "My root lama, the embodiment of all lineages ..." you should visualize Buddha Amitabha above you as the embodiment of your root guru and all lineage gurus since Buddha Vajradhara. It is very important to practice this because you make a connection with the blessings of refuge. It is through these blessings of the lamas and lineage gurus that one attains any benefit from the practice. When doing this practice, have confidence in your lama and the lineage, in their realization, their enlightened mind, and their compassionate mind, and then surely blessings will come and help you actualize your practice.

Now, in this context, you may visualize whoever your lama happens to be, with whom you have a very special connection, devotion, faith, and confidence. For example, you may have a personal connection with His Holiness the Dalai Lama; that is your lama who is the most beneficial source of spiritual understanding for you. Remember, it is your root guru but in the appearance of Buddha Amitabha.

When you recite this refuge prayer, you invoke the blessings to descend through the line of lineage gurus, starting all the way back from Samantabhadra, the primoridal Buddha, then to Vajrasattva, then Garab Dorje, and so on to the Tibetan lama lineage holders and down to our root guru; and finally they all dissolve into one another. For example, they then dissolve into His Holiness The Dalai Lama, Tenzin Gyatso, who is the essence of all the gurus appearing as Buddha Amitabha. So with this kind of visualization, intense transmission occurs, delivering the blessings of all these lineage gurus to whom you have such gratitude. That is how important it is when you say the prayer of refuge and visualize the blessings flowing through your lineage gurus.

Kusuli Chöd

Kusuli Chöd originates from the Longchen Nyingthig tradition. It encompasses the same meaning as its sister practice, the Khandro Gye Kyang, or The Dakini's Laughter, but it is shorter and easier to practice. It is meant for yogis and yoginis, living in the midst of everyday life. It is simple, with no need for altars, offerings, or shrines. All you need your own body as offering. Thus it is a very straightforward and profound practice.

Yogis and yoginis who have entered a path of renunciation have no families or homes. They take their shelter under trees, in caves, or in any corner they can find. They don't stay in one spot very long; they live free of material possessions. Wandering here and there, their purpose in life is to help people wherever there is a need. Such great practitioners go to places where they know they can assist others, and they do so without being asked. They cure illnesses and relieve suffering, and their primary method of helping is through this practice called Chöd. They offer their bodies to the demonic forces and disturbed energies that are causing harm to others in order to benefit beings according to their specific ailments.

The Elements of Life

The suffering of sentient beings, physically or otherwise, is generally caused by grasping at the notion of self (dak dzin). This attachment to self, combined with harmful negative forces, is the cause of our mental and/or physical suffering. Physical suffering in particular is caused by an imbalance of the elements.

How does this come about?

First, we need to understand the meanings of the five elements. Each element corresponds to a color and a cardinal direction.

Corresponding to the east and the color white, the Water element gives rise to all the fluids in our bodies, such as our blood and mucus. In the south, the yellow Earth element corresponds to our solid structure, such as the bones and flesh. In the west, the red Fire element governs our heat and warmth. In the north, the green Wind element relates to our breath, lungs, and movement of energy in the body. The blue Space element in the center, is open potential itself, and it relates to our consciousness.

When these elements are in balance, we are considered healthy. If the Fire element is high and the Water element is low, you will suffer from fever or a heat-related disease. If the Earth element is low and the Wind element is high, you will feel stressed out or nervous. If the Space element is not in harmony with the other elements, emotional and mental illnesses arise.

When the elements are disturbed, not only is the body ill, but there are also psychological effects. Excessive Water element promotes desire, while excessive Earth element promotes hatred. Fire element gives rise to pride, and the northern, green-colored Wind element generates jealousy. Finally, a disturbed Space element causes delusion and confusion. Great accomplished yogis, known as kusuli, understand that suffering is caused by these imbalances; through the power of their meditation, they seek to balance the energy of suffering beings.

In recognizing the true nature of these elements, the Water element is seen as Buddha Vajrasattva, and the yellow Earth element is Buddha Ratnasambava. Fire in the west is known to be Buddha Amitabha. The green Wind element in the north is actually Amogasiddhi. Finally, blue Space energy is recognized as Vairocana. If one perceives and understands that one's own body is none other than these five Buddhas, one will perceive the body as extremely precious and holy.

In the heart chakra reside forty-two peaceful deities, while in the crown chakra dwell fifty-eight wrathful deities. Thus, our bodies contain one hundred peaceful and wrathful sacred beings. Each one, enshrined in our body, is contained within a seed syllable. And the seed syllables of these hundred deities correspond to the hundred-syllable mantra of Vajrasattva.

In Chöd practice, the yogi recognizes that people suffer because of disturbing emotions and imbalanced elements. He offers his own body and mind to the demons that are causing the problems. The demons are drawn to his profound example as a practitioner, and they flock to the yogi who commits fully to this practice.

Thus, when a kusuli yogi performs a healing, he will communicate with the demons or negative forces. At the same time, he is conscious that the demons inhabit a body that *simultaneously enshrines a hundred deities*. Because these negative forces are harming not just the person but also the enshrined deities, they are accumulating negative karma – thus the yogi offers his body and flesh as a substitute for the negative forces to consume.

Feast Preparation

Going for refuge and generating bodhicitta are an indispensible part of any Chöd practice. In this case we visualize a HUM syllable in your heart that instantly becomes Vajravarahi, (Troma Nagmo), the wrathful Machig Lapdron. Keeping in mind that she represents your own essential awareness, she is luminous and brilliantly radiating light. This light shines out and calls for the actual Troma Nagmo to come and abide in your heart, thus merging your own innate awareness with that of the enlightened awareness of the deity. In this way take refuge and generate Bodhicitta.

PHAT

The syllable PHAT[3] is the essence of the Prajnaparamita, the "Perfection of Wisdom." All Tantric mantras are condensed into the syllables PHA and TA, and the combination of the two is PHAT. When uttered, the sound of the syllable PHAT has a powerful effect, because it is the essence of all the Sutras and Tantras. If one feels afraid at any time, for example while alone in the wilderness or in a big empty house, seeing hallucinations or hearing things, just saying PHAT can dispel all fear and anxiety, leaving you in peace.

---

[3] www.visiblemantra.org for other examples of Tibetan and Sanskrit calligraphy.

PHAT has many meanings and actions. During preparation of the Chöd feast, the kusuli yogi pronounces PHAT, and visualizes his consciousness being ejected through the central channel and out of the crown of his head into the space above him. He takes on the form of wrathful Vajravarahi, as large as can be imagined. The ordinary body, with no consciousness, is then conceived to fall down lifeless in the space in front. He then visualizes three huge skulls, representing the three kayas, and the three times – past, present and future. The three skulls are arranged like a tripod to form a hearth.

From the heart of the Vajravahi, another dakini appears, holding a curved knife. She descends and touches the forehead of one's lifeless corpse, cutting it open to form a skullcup. The skullcup becomes large enough to contain the three realms of existence and rests on the tripod of skulls. With her left hand, she then throws the rest of the body into the vast container.

Under the skullcup is a Tibetan letter AH, while above is a white Tibetan letter HA. As the yogi recites OM AH HUM, a fire is produced underneath the skullcup, and it melts the body into an ocean of nectar. From the heated contents, a bluish-red steam rises up, its warmth melting the HA above, causing white nectar to drip down and mix with the contents of the skullcap. The result is a vast sacred substance that can fulfill all wishes and desires. The OM makes the skull cup huge, AH transforms the nectar and the HUM makes the contents of the cup inexhaustible so that it can always fulfill the wishes and desires of all beings.

OM AH HUNG

The Offering

The yogi, still in the form of Vajravarahi, recites the three syllables OM AH HUM over and over. These symbolize the perfect body, speech, and mind of all enlightened beings – as well as the body, speech, and mind of ordinary beings, including those of the harming forces. While reciting, he visualizes making offerings to the Buddhas' body, speech, and mind, starting with the primordial Buddha Samantabhadra, all the way down the lineage to the yogi's root guru. This is continued until the Buddhas are completely satisfied, then they send back blessings in the form of light from their head, throat and heart. The light dissolves back into the skull cup making the contents of the cup very powerful. Remember that the reason we make offerings to the Buddhas and Bodhisattvas is not because they are hungry or have any particular needs; it is simply done to accumulate merit for the benefit of oneself or for the suffering person.

Then similar offerings are made to the protectors and deities from the four categories of Tantras, such as Chakrasamvara, Hevajra and Yamantaka. This is for generating accomplishments or siddhis in one's own practice. Then offerings are made to the Protectors such as Mahakala, and also to the Worldly Guardians such as Shiva, Brahma, and Vishnu, asking them to protect sentient beings from natural catastrophes, famine, and other unfavorable circumstances. In particular, they agree to protect your mediation practice from interferences.

Next, the yogi invites the Nagas, or serpentine water beings, who are worthy of receiving your offerings. They are particularly pleased by offerings of milk and sandalwood. There are two categories of Nagas – those who are suitable to be invited, and those who are not.

The latter kind cannot be invited as guests because their mere presence can cause harm to the other guests. Such Nagas can spread epidemics and illnesses. Some carry contagious diseases on their breath, while others cause illnesses just by touching other beings. Therefore they have to keep their distance from other beings. For these Nagas, the yogi emanates many different offering goddesses from the heart of Vajravarahi, who delivers the offerings to them.

There are four categories of invisible beings who are always too busy to come when invited, and they are almost comical in nature. One is called Chara. Chara is extremely worried that all the wealth in the universe will be stolen. He spends all of his time guarding over gold and other precious metals. No one appointed him to this position, but because of his karma, he is constantly concerned and worried about losing it.

There is another being called Lagring, which literally means "Long Arm." He believes that Mt. Meru, the largest mountain in the universe, is going to topple over, and so he is constantly trying to hold it up. Another being named Shongto lives in a cottage by a lake next to Mt. Meru. He is worried that an earthquake will dislodge a boulder from Mt. Meru, and that the boulder will roll into the lake and cause a flood that will wash away his cottage! So he spends all of his time scooping water out of the lake to prevent the flood. These beings, because of their karma, focus on these irrational worries. Understanding that these beings have no time to come and participate in the feast, the yogi sends food to them out of compassion.

There are also harmful spirits of a parasitic nature who feed off the flesh and blood of others. The yogi or yogini invites them and makes offerings to them as well. They are asked to take as much as they can, even to take food away with them if they can carry it. The yogi's offerings and compassionate concern pacify their harmful attitudes, and their greed and anger.

The next offerings are directed toward all the sentient beings of the Six Realms. The yogi visualizes that the nectar in the skullcup – his transformed body – turns into whatever it is that beings need and desire. Human beings have many wishes and desires, food, clothing, companionship, wealth and so forth. We visualize offering goddesses bringing all humans exactly what they desire. If they want a boyfriend or girlfriend, then this is delivered. If they want a new car, then this is delivered. Upon receiving these things, they become completely satisfied and are happy.

Next, all animals are visualized as being freed from their stupidity, and freed from being hunted, enslaved, or eaten. After that, the yogi visualizes humans liberated from grasping, longing, and clinging. They receive whatever they wish for: If they want a house, this is given to them; if they wish for a car, they obtain it; if they are wanting a son or daughter, this is offered to them. Whatever humans need and desire, the yogi emanates different dakinis from his heart, and the dakinis bring these offerings to the humans.

Next focus on the hungry ghosts who exist in many varieties. Some have huge bellies with a small throat, so they cannot eat easily. Another kind have big bellies, but their necks are knotted, preventing them from eating and swallowing. These unfortunate beings suffer because of their intense greed in the past. Those with knots in their throats, for example, may have prevented others from practicing generosity, such as dissuading a rich man from giving to a charity by saying, "Don't do that, it's a waste of money!"

Through these offerings, all of the guests are satisfied, in particular, you have satisfied samsaric beings who wonder from life to life – thinking that their karmic debts are purified. Beings who cause harm are purified and no longer cause harm. See all of these illnesses causing spirits dissolving into emptiness, sunyata. When practicing for oneself, see any kind of interference or obstacle dissolve into emptiness. In particular, the cause of our affliction is our clinging to a false notion of self. By dissolving this too into emptiness, the sphere of giver, receiver and gift dissolve into the primordial expression of AH. The AH syllable expresses the perfection of wisdom.

Using Chöd for Healing

This practice can be used to heal sick people, repair environments and generally be very helpful. When doing Chöd for others, the words and format stays the same, but the visualization changes.

After performing the refuge and bodhicitta as before, you eject the consciousness of the person or people of your compassion. When doing this, visualize an AH syllable in their heart(s), then when you say PHAT, eject the AH from their central channel, as described in the previous Powa teaching. Their consciousness merges into Vajravarahi, who is also yourself.

When making the offerings to the guests, in this case you use the sick person's body in the skull cup to be transformed into nectar. When you do this, make offerings to the upper guests, the blessings are returned to them. The offerings to the lower guests are to repay the other person's karmic debt, clearing them of their own harmful spirits. This practice can have tremendous benefit for these people, and they wont even know how it happened.

Remember that at the end of the practice, dissolve their consciousness back into their body and consider that they have been completely healed and that their minds are in a very calm, altruistic state. Feel joy that you have been able to help them!

Expanding Benefit

Through their enlightened motivation, great practitioners are able to make offerings of their own bodies. The ability to do this is an indication of the meditator's higher advancement. The practice not only benefits others, but also carries the entire line of Buddha's blessings, from the Dharmakaya down through the lineage masters. Whoever feels these blessings experiences a profound sense of peace, and easily generates the mind of love and compassion. The beings who taste the offerings immediately become free from their anger, jealousy, and other afflictions.

Practitioners who have engaged for a long time in this practice actually become a powerful source of meaning, such that their bodies, speech, and minds become beneficial to others. For example, even their touch or just the sound of their voice can help others instantly. Either through visualization or in physical reality, just the taste of their offerings brings immense peace and healing. This principle of liberation and healing through tasting, hearing, and touching explains why, when a great yogi recites prayers such as "OM AH HUM VAJRA GURU PEMA SIDDHI HUM," it causes those who hear it to feel great ease and happiness, releasing their suffering.

When great masters, Buddhas, Bodhisattvas, and accomplished realized yogis touch you, this can heal and even liberate you. This is why, in the Tibetan tradition, great masters touch people as a form of healing and blessing. With faith, the mere sight of blessed images of Buddhas or Bodhisattvas, and great masters such as the Dalai Lama, can bring one great joy. Statues that have been properly blessed can have a similar effect.

All phenomena arise out of causes. For positive outcomes, one must give birth to confidence and other positive psychological states. Enlightened beings have no partiality; their compassion extends to all beings, no matter who they are. But those receiving these blessings should also have confidence and the correct motivation for the maximum effect – otherwise the benefit is limited. If we need help and relief from suffering, we must sustain both certainty and devotion. Like a circular ring, one's faith can be "hooked" by the blessings of the deities and the skillful practitioner. Being without faith and devotion is like having an iron ball instead of an open ring – the hook of blessings can never catch on to it.

Thus if we visualize one hundred Buddha Shakyamunis or Vajrayoginis above or within us – without faith – it is just useless. If we visualize even one deity with full faith, it is like having countless numbers of them around us. This is analogous to the idea of a hundred cups set out in the sun. If ninety-nine of them are filled with water, each will contain a reflection of the sun. However, if one cup is empty of water, of faith, no sun will appear. If one's aspirations and confidence are correct, then whatever you do, your life becomes spiritual practice and accumulates wholesome merit. It is thus that we need to watch and be careful about our attitudes.

Practice and Daily Life

When doing this practice, never be separated from an altruistic motivation, with feelings of love, compassion and generosity.

In ancient India there were many great Mahasiddhas, accomplished masters. One of them, named Tilopa, used to pound sesame seeds, to extract its oil to sell. He was young and very diligent in his work. One day he met a very learned and accomplished Mahasiddha. Tilopa asked the Mahasiddha about his special qualities. The Mahasiddha replied that he was a meditator. Tilopa then asked him what kind of meditation he did. The Mahasiddha told him that he meditated on the Tantric deity Chakrasamvara. The boy Tilopa asked how he could do a similar meditation.

"What do you do for a living?" asked the Master.

"I extract oil from sesame seeds and sell it," replied Tilopa.

"So in your profession, what do you think of most when you go to bed? And in the morning when you go to sell your product, what is in your mind?"

Tilopa said, "When I go to bed, I am always thinking about where I can find more good seeds. In the morning when I go to sell my oil, I am thinking about where to go to get the best price. These are my constant thoughts day and night."

So the master said, "That is fine, but I can teach you a technique so that it becomes a meditation."

The boy asked, "How is that?"

"The trick to your practice is this: Instead of worrying at night about how to acquire seeds that have lots of oil, go to bed thinking that all sentient beings are your mothers and fathers, and so that they can have a good meal, you'd like to bring them good oil to cook with. In the morning when you go to sell your oil, do not be lazy – go out thinking that your fathers and mothers are waiting for you to help them. Because you are healthy and energetic, you will be diligent in supplying them with the oil and bringing it to them so they can have their meals."

The Master further instructed that Tilopa should sell the oil to them and accept whatever price they could afford to pay him, without bargaining, no matter who it was. He should not think of profits, said the Master, but always regard his business or job as a service for all sentient beings who are suffering. In that way, Tilopa would have his business, and at the same time, his meditation. With such an attitude he would be able to accomplish his practice of Chakrasamvara and one day attain a vision of the deity.

The boy Tilopa practiced as instructed, and after twelve years he truly had a vision of the deity Chakrasamvara. The Buddha Chakrasamvara said to him, "You have attained and perfected wholesome merits, and you have purified the two aspects of defilements and obscurations; the gross defilements of afflictions and the subtle defilements of conceptual thinking. Now you are truly enlightened. You need not do your work any more; instead you should meditate and go to the Pure Land."

Tilopa, whose name "Tilo" means "he who sells sesame," could then physically go to the pure realm of Oddiyana, where he received teachings directly from Vajradhara, the primordial Buddha. Vajradhara gave him the instructions on Vajrayogini. Tilopa later gave the transmission to Naropa, who gave them to the Tibetan Marpa, who then bestowed them on Milarepa and so on down through the the lamas of the lineage, and now we have the teachings today.

Whatever one's profession or job is, if one does it with the right motivation, and the correct attitude, it becomes a practice of dharma. Likewise, we should do the chöd practice with such motivation.

Questions & Answers

Question: How can we understand the wrathful deities and the connection between the wrathful deities and the negative afflictions?

Lama Wangdu: In order to fully understand the significance of the wrathful aspects, one needs to study extensively from the foundation. There are many teachings and commentaries related to this subject. After you receive teachings and instructions, practicing them will help you understand what they are really like. This understanding will come from your own experience.

Question: Could you explain what you mean by the Three Realms?

LW: According to Buddhism, there are three realms of beings. Above our human realm live the gods, where there are thirty-two levels. The four continents span the universe according to Buddhist cosmology, and in the center stands Mt. Meru, which has different stories. On the fourth level are the four guardian gods, and atop this are four elephants standing below the god realm. The surface of the head of the elephant is as big as the earth itself, with many cities and towns. In the center of the elephant head is a turquoise field, and in the middle of that turquoise field is the celestial palace of the King of the Gods. Here it is completely peaceful and beautiful, and there is no shortage of anything with abundance, prosperity, and happiness all over. The gods there emit light from their bodies and they have no worries.

Below this is the realm of humans, sentient beings like ourselves, with the continent of the human realms and the other continents that are similar to Earth. In these worlds, we have ups and downs, and sufferings related to birth, aging, sickness, and death. Some countries are poor, some are rich; some lands are hostile and some are pleasant. We go through life with hopes and expectations and doubts and fears.

From the god realms, different divine beings manifest on the earth realm and try to guide and help us. There are also manifestations and emanations of Buddhas and bodhisattvas appearing within the human realm to teach and guide beings onto the path that will lead to happiness and freedom from suffering. This is what we call the human realm.

Below that, and under the water, are the realms of the nagas. The naga realms are supposedly very wealthy, with gems and precious substances, yet they are poor in spiritual practice. They have a great longing and wish to understand the teachings and practice of Buddha.

Buddhas and bodhisattvas, as well as many divine beings from the god realms, can travel to the naga realms and teach dharma there. So this is what is meant by the three realms of existence.

Question: I thought Tilopa was a fisherman?

LW: Before he became Tilopa the Master, he had to work selling oil. After he became a master, he was not a fisherman, but he ate a lot of fish. When he became a very accomplished practitioner, he lived a very unconventional life, wearing dirty clothes and not caring about his appearance or status. He would sit in a corner, frying and eating fish thrown away by fishermen. Occasionally his sister would help him. But each fish that he ate, he would liberate and transfer it to the pure land.

Another master and scholar named Naropa heard about Tilopa, and this instantly gave rise to great devotion in his heart. So he went to search for him.

Naropa inquired of the people he met, "Have you ever seen the master Tilopa? Where can I find him?"

The local people were not aware of how enlightened Tilopa was. They considered him just a vagabond beggar who ate leftover fish. So the locals told Naropa, "We don't know of any great Master named Tilopa, but we do know of a beggar named Tilopa. You will find him in the corner there."

So Naropa went where they had indicated, and he saw a very dirty old Indian, frying fish alive and eating them. He thought to himself, "That couldn't possibly be the master Tilopa, the enlightened one." He had a little doubt.

Tilopa instantly read his mind, covered his body with leftover cloth, and snapped his fingers, whereby the fish turned into rainbows. Tilopa then turned his back to Naropa.

Naropa now realized how accomplished Tilopa was, and he asked Tilopa's forgiveness. He asked to be taken as his disciple. But Tilopa refused to talk to him.

Nearby in a small stream were many leeches. People would jump over the stream in order to get accross. Tilopa began walking up and down the bank of the stream, pretending that he really wished to cross but couldn't jump. Naropa asked him, "Can't you just jump over it? If not I will lie down and make a bridge for you."

So he stretched himself over to make a bridge. As Tilopa walked on him very slowly, many leeches attached themselves to Naropa's body.

He lost so much blood that he fainted. Tilopa asked him, "What's the problem?"

Naropa said, "I think I'm quite dead!"

When Tilopa waved his hand over Naropa's body, he instantly came back to health.

Naropa then asked Tilopa to teach him dharma. So Tilopa asked him to go for a walk. He took his new student to climb up a building over 20 stories high. From the top Tilopa looked down and asked Naropa, "Do you really think there is anybody who can really listen to their Lama?"

Naropa said, "Surely I can!"

"Then jump."

So Naropa jumped. At the bottom, he was badly injured with broken bones. Tilopa came down to him, waved his hand, and restored him back to normal, asking, "Was it very painful?"

"Oh not only painful, but I think I died."

"Yes indeed, you were dead."

They then visited a wedding ceremony. The groom was well dressed and the bride was covered in flower garlands. There was music, and many people were dancing.

Tilopa was watching the ceremony, and Naropa asked, "What are you looking at?"

Tilopa said, "I also need a wife, that one right there in fact. Would you bring her to me?"

So Naropa went and grabbed the bride. Naturally, the wedding guests attacked him when he did that. Some of them had sticks, and they beat him to a pulp.Naropa was almost dead. Again, Tilopa came to him, waved his hand, and restored him back to health.

Naropa underwent a total of twelve such dangerous ordeals, called "Naropa's Twelve Trials." After these twelve trials, Naropa again asked Tilopa for dharma instruction.

"So do you really want these dharma teachings?" asked Tilopa. Naropa nodded. Tilopa, who always wore wooden sandals, took one off and slapped Naropa hard on his face, knocking him unconscious. But when he woke up, he had attained the complete realization and all the wisdom of Tilopa.

These where the days when masters could teach disciples, transmitting realization like pouring water from one vessel into another. This is unlike our selves today, who need to have empowerments, transmissions, and all these other activities.

Naropa and Tilopa had equal realization. Tilopa's sister, who was often with him and helped care for him, also had realization.

When Tilopa was ninety he left his mortal body, leaving his instructions and transmissions to Naropa.

Naropa had many disciples who were accomplished. One was the Tibetan, Marpa the translator, along with the Pamtingpa brothers from Nepal. To the Nepali disciples Naropa gave the transmission of the

Vajrayogini practices. To Marpa he gave the four classes of tantra, primarily the transmission of Vajravarahi.

This concludes my explanation on Kusuli Chöd, the basis for understanding Chöd, what to visualize, and how to bring the practice into your daily life.

Long Life Prayer for Lama Wangdu

༄༅།།ཞབས་བརྟན་གསོལ་འདེབས་དད་པའི་དབྱངས་སྙན་བཞུགས་སོ།།

The Sweet Melodious Song of Faith
A Long-Life Prayer for Lama Tsering Wangdu

ཨོཾ་སྭ་སྟི།

OM SO TI
OM SO TI

སྐྱབས་གནས་དཀོན་མཆོག་གསུམ་ལ་ཕྱག་འཚལ་ལོ།

KYAB NE KON CHOG SUM LA CHAG TSEL LO
Homage to the three Jewels of Refuge,

།རྒྱ་གར་འཕགས་ཡུལ་སྐྱེས་ཆེན་མཁས་གྲུབ་གནས།

GYA GAR PAG YUL KYE CHEN KE DRUB NE
In noble India, place of saints and sages,

།སྟོན་པའི་ལུང་བཞིན་འོད་ཟེར་འབུམ་དང་བཅས།

TON PAY LUNG ZHIN Ö ZER BUM DANG CHE
Born according to Buddha's prophecy, with a hundred thousand light rays,

།གྲུབ་པའི་དབང་ཕྱུག་ཉི་བདུན་དབང་པོ་བཞིན།

DRUB PAY WANG CHUG TA DUN WANG PO ZHIN
The sovereign lord of siddhas rose like the sun,

།མཐའ་འཁོབ་བོད་ཀྱི་མུན་པ་གསལ་བྱེད་དུ།

TA KOB BÖ KYI MUN PA SEL JE DU
Dispelling the darkness of the primitive border-land of Tibet,

།ཡ་གཅིག་དམ་པ་སངས་རྒྱས་དངོས་སུ་བྱོན།

PA CHIG DAM PA SANG GYE NGO SU JON
Holy father Dampa Sangye had truly arrived.

།ཞིང་སྐྱོང་མཁའ་འགྲོའི་ཕོ་བྲང་གླང་འཁོར་དུ།

ZHING KYONG KA DRÖ PO DRANG LANG KOR DU
At Langkor, the fortress of worldly protectors and Dakinis,

།སྡུག་བསྔལ་ཞི་བྱེད་ཆོས་ཀྱི་འཁོར་ལོ་བསྐོར།

DUG NGEL ZHI JE CHÖ KYI KOR LO KOR
He turned the wheel of the Dharma of Shijay—the Pacification of

Suffering,

།གྲངས་ལས་འདས་པ་སྨིན་གྲོལ་ལམ་དུ་བཀོད།

DRANG LE DE PA MIN DROL LAM DU KO
Placing beings beyond measure on the path of ripening and liberation.

།གྲུབ་ཐོབ་ཕོ་མོ་ཆུ་བོའི་རྒྱུན་བཞིན་བྱུང་།

DRUB TOB PO MO CHU WÖ GYUN ZHIN JUNG
Male and female siddhas sprang forth like a flowing river.

།མཐའ་འཁོབ་བོད་འདི་ཆོས་ལྡན་ཞིང་དུ་བསྒྱུར།

TA KOB BÖ DI CHÖ DEN ZHING DU GYUR
And the savage land of Tibet became a place of Dharma.

208

ཨི་ཕྱིད་དད་པའི་བཀའ་དྲིན་རྗེས་སུ་དྲན།

MI CHE DE PAY KA DRIN JE SU DREN
We remember your kindness with unswerving faith.

སླར་ཡང་གངས་ལྗོངས་སྐྱེ་འགྲོའི་བསོད་ནམས་སུ།

LAR YANG GANG JONG KYE DRO SO NAM SU
Later, to bring merit to the beings of the Land of Snow,

གྲུབ་ཐོབ་རྣམ་གསུམ་སྤྲུན་འདྲེན་སྐལ་བཟང་ཤར།

DRUB TOB NAM SUM CHEN DREN KEL ZANG SHAR

Good fortunate arose, and three Siddhas were brought forth.

དམ་པའི་སྐུ་རྟེན་གསེར་ཞལ་འཛུམ་ཆན་འདི།

DAM PAY KU TEN SER ZHEL TZUM CHEN DI
When people, high or low, encountered the smiling golden face of
Padampa's statue,

སྐྱེ་བོ་མཆོག་དམན་སུ་ཡིས་མཇལ་ཙམ་ནོ།

KEY WO CHOG MEN SU YI JEL TSAM NO
The blessing was so great that it made their hair stand on end with faith.

དད་པའི་སྤུ་ལོང་རྒྱས་པའི་བྱིན་རླབས་ཆེ།

DE PAY PU LONG GYE PAY JIN LAB CHE
This is a banquet laid out for inviting Padampa in reality!

དམ་པ་དངོས་སུ་བྱོན་པའི་དགའ་སྟོན་གཤོམ།

DAM PA NGO SU JON PAY GA TON SHOM
And he who made the dharma offering of erecting this form,

209

ཁེ་འདྲའི་སྐུ་རྟེན་བཞིངས་མཁན་ཆོས་སྦྱིན་ནི།

DE DRAY KU TEN ZHENG KEN CHÖ JIN NI

Has spent his entire life in practice, traveling and staying in charnel
grounds.

ཚེ་གཅིག་གྲུབ་དང་དུར་ཁྲོད་བསྐོར་ནས་བཞུགས།

TSE CHIG DRUB DANG DUR TRO KOR NE ZHUG

Dwelling in the city, he works one-pointedly,

གྲོང་ན་གནས་ཚེ་ཉིན་མཚན་དབྱེར་མེད་དུ།

DRONG NA NE TSE NYIN TSEN YER ME DU

To benefit the sick and the dead,

རྗེ་གཅིག་ནད་དང་གཤིན་པོའི་དོན་དུ་གཞོལ།

TSE CHIG NE DANG SHIN PO DÖN DU ZHOL

day and night,

རིས་མེད་ཀུན་གྱི་བདེ་སྡུག་མ་ལྟར་གཟིགས།

RI ME KUN GYI DE DUG MA TAR ZIG

Like a mother who looks impartially on joy and suffering.

བྱམས་དང་སྙིང་རྗེའི་བདག་ཉིད་བྱང་སེམས་མཆོག

JAM DANG NYING JE DAG NYI JANG SEM CHOG

The very nature of love and compassion, Supreme Bodhicitta,

དོན་དུ་གྲུབ་པའི་དབང་ཕྱུག་ཆེན་པོ་སྟེ།

DON DU DRUB PAY WANG CHUG CHEN PO TE

Accomplishing life's meaning, the great powerful being,

ཚུར་མཐོང་སྐྱེ་བོའི་ཚོགས་ལ་ཡོངས་སུ་ནི།

TSUR TONG KYE PÖ TSOG LA YONG SU NI
Who was born among ordinary samsaric folk,

ངུར་སྨྲིག་འཛིན་པའི་དབང་འདུས་བླ་མ་གྲགས།

NGUR MIG TZIN PAY WANG DU LA MA DRAG
Became renowned as Wangdu Lama, holder of the saffron-robes.

དམ་པའི་སྐུ་རྟེན་བཞིངས་པས་བསོད་ནམས་མཐུས།

DAM PAY KU TEN ZHENG PE SO NAM TU
By the force of the merit of erecting these statues,

གྲུབ་དབང་ཆེན་པོ་སྐུ་ཚེ་རབ་བརྟན་ཤོག

DRUB WANG CHEN PO KU TSE RAB TEN SHOG
May the great and powerful siddha's life remain unshakeable.

གང་གི་འཕྲིན་ལས་ཕྱོགས་བཅུར་རྒྱས་པར་ཤོག

GANG GI TRIN LE CHOG CHUR GYE PAR SHOG
May his Buddha activity spread in the ten directions;

དཀར་ཕྱོགས་ལྷ་རྣམས་དགྱེས་པའི་རྟེན་འབྲེལ་ཤོག

KAR CHOG LHA NAM GYE PAY TEN DREL SHOG
May pleasing the Deities on the side of goodness create an auspicious

connection;

ཡིད་ཅན་ཀུན་གྱི་དུག་གསུམ་རབ་ཞི་ནས།

YI CHEN KUN GYI DUG SUM RAB SHI NE
Through completely pacifiying the three poisons of all conscious beings,

ཁཐར་ཐུག་མྱང་འདས་གོ་འཕང་འཐོབ་པར་ཤོག

TAR TUG NYANG DE GO PANG TOB PAR SHOG
May they attain the final goal of Nirvana.

ཁབདག་ཅག་སྙིང་ནས་བསྐུལ་བའི་གསོལ་བ་དག

DAG CHAG NYING NE KUL WAY SÖL WA DAG
May the heart felt prayers of myself and others,

ཁདད་སྨོན་མཐུ་ཡིས་འགྲུབ་པའི་བཀྲ་ཤིས་ཤོག

DE MON TU YI DRUB PAY TA SHI SHOG
Be accomplished through the force of our faith and devotion, and may all

be auspicious!

སྨོས་པ།

Dedication

ཐེབ་སྐོར་རྒྱན་སོགས་སྐོས་པ་མི་མངའ་ཡང་།

DEB CHOR KYEN SO DRO PA MI NGA YANG
It is without metaphor to ornament this prayer…

ཁསྨན་ལྗོངས་པུར་རྒྱལ་བོད་ཀྱི་དཔལ་ཉིད་དུ།

MEN JONG PUR GYAL BÖ KYI PEL NYI DU
For the glorious medicine land of Tibet,

ཁརིམ་ཕྲོན་འཕགས་བོད་བསྟན་འཛིན་མཁས་གྲུབ་དང་།

RIM CHON PAG BÖ TEN DZIN KHA DRUP DANG
To the success of Dharma lineage holders of Tibet and India,

།བདག་ཆག་སློབ་དཔོན་བཀའ་དྲིན་གསབ་པའི་ཕྱིར།

DAG CHAG LOB PÖN KA DRIN SAB PA'I CHIR
And for the repayment of the kindness of my lamas,

།མེ་ཏོག་ཆུང་ཡང་ལྷ་རྫས་དཔེ་ཇི་བཞིན།

ME TOG CHUNG YANG LHA DZE PE JI SHIN
Although my flower is so small, it is as the offerings substances of the

Gods,

།དད་པའི་རང་སྐུལ་ཚེ་ཆུ་ཚོགས་པ་ནས།

DE PA'I RANG KUL TSE CHU TSOK PA NE
By the devotion from our spontaneous requests as practitioners,

།ཚིག་ཚོགས་ལམ་ནས་ལ་དོལ་འདི་ལྟར་ཐལ།

TSIG TSOG LAM NE LA DOL DI TAR THEL
With these collected words, I praise the lamas.

།ནོངས་པ་ཐམས་ཅད་མཆོག་གསུམ་སྤྱན་སྔར་བཤགས།

NONG PA THAM CHE CHOG SUM CHEN NGAR SHAG
I confess and regret in front of the three supreme ones.

།སྨན་པ་ཏིལ་འབྲུ་བྱུང་ཡང་དགེ་བར་བསྔོ།

MEN PA DIL TRU CHUNG YANG GE WAR NGO
Even though I have accumulated only a sesame seed size amount of

benefit, I dedicated this virtue.

།སརྦ་མངྒ་ལཾཿ

SARVA MANGALAM
May all be happy!